Table of contents

My Story

30 days to my purpose

Chapter 1

Day 1-15

Birthday in jail

Chapter 2

Day 16-18

My Pet Spider

Chapter 3

Day 19-23

Seeing a man facing LIFE

Chapter 4

Day 24-29

Eve of my last 30 days in jail

Conclusion

Day 30

Jail Summary

MY STORY

I started to write about my life, which included my childhood, teenage years, then all the way up to now. I realized people have heard stories like mine many times. To sum it all up in a nut shell. At the time of writing this book,

I'm 48 years old with a bad drinking problem in which I'm in jail for now. I'm a only child raised by my mother, no father figure in my life, I was shamed of the way I looked, didn't have a lot of clothes or friends, always worried what people thought of me etc.

On top of all that. I was raised in the church or you could say; I was in the church but not of the church. I had my first drink at 5 years of age.

NOW YOU GET IT? I SURE HOPE SO. FOR ALL MY DRINKING TROUBLES I NEVER SPENT ANY REAL TIME IN JAIL OR EVEN WENT TO PRISON. THAT'S ALL CHANGED, I'M DOING SOME REAL TIME NOW. THIS HAS TO BE MY LAST RODEO AS THE SAYING GOES. BUT WHATS GOING TO BE DIFFERENT FROM ALL THE OTHER TIMES I'VE BEEN IN TROUBLE, YOU MAY ASK.

A LOT OF PEOPLE FIND GOD OR RELIGION WHEN IN SERIOUS TROUBLE, IN JAIL OR PRISON. THATS 99.9% TRUE. IN MOST PEOPLES FILES OR SITUATIONS, THEY HAVE NO REAL SERIOUS PROBLEMS AND LIVING WELL FINANCIALLY, PHYSICALLY AN MENTALLY.

IT WILL BE HARD FOR GOD TO GET ONES ATTENTION IF AT ALL WHEN EVERYTHING IS GOING WELL. GOD WILL LET YOU PUT YOURSELF IN SITUATIONS WHERE NO AMOUNT OF MONEY OR ANYONE CAN HELP YOU. THEN YOU HAVE TO REALIZE, GOD IS ALL YOU NEED CAUSE GOD IS ALL YOU GOT.

You're now force to lean on him(God) for help. Now he's got your attention. God loves us so much and wants us to be a part of his kingdom to love and praise him.

In return he lets us live a blessed life here on earth but most of all have eternal life in heaven with him. Being raised in the church I knew all this but strayed(backslid) away from him. I'm thankful for being able to come back to him and be a part of his kingdom.

Most don't get that chance. Satan destroys them till they can't see their way back or kill them. God has showed me, we can't make it without him.

We have to make him the center of our life. This will insure a blessed life for us all. If we don't live a Christ-centered life, we can be facing prison and death.

1Peter 5:8 says:
Be sober, be vigilant; because your adversary the devil, as a roaring lion, walks about, seeking whom he may devour.

I LOOK AT IT LIKE THIS; MY LIFE IS AT STAKE AND GOD ALLOWED SATAN TO TARE ME DOWN SO HE(GOD) CAN BUILD ME BACK UP FOR HIS GLORY. EVEN THOUGH I HAVE A ROUGH ROAD AHEAD OF ME. I KNOW I'LL BE OK AS LONG AS GOD IS IN THE DRIVER SEAT.

Matt 6:33:
But seek first his kingdom l and his righteousness, and all these things will be given to you.

Never stop believing in yourself . God has not.

30 DAYS TO MY PURPOSE

(Ephesians 3:18)

May be able to comprehend with all saints what is the breadth, and length, and depth, and height.

THIS IS AN ACCOUNT OF MY LAST 30 DAYS IN JAIL. I'M WRITING THIS IN HOPES OF HELPING THE ONES WHO ARE INCARCERATE. I'LL BE WILL TELLING MY THOUGHTS, FEARS, WORRIES, GOD, DOUBTS, FEELINGS OF LONELINESS ETC.

I'M REALLY HOPING THE THINGS I SAY CAN BE RELATED TO YOU IN YOUR SITUATION. SO WHEN YOU GET TO YOUR LAST 30 DAYS OF INCARCERATION, YOU'LL KNOW THAT YOU'RE NOT THE FIRST OR THE LAST TO GO THROUGH THIS. ALSO IN THE PROCESS YOU'LL LEARN THERE'S A PURPOSE FOR YOUR LIFE ON A LEVEL YOU CAN'T IMAGINE.

I HOPE YOU CAN REALIZE IT THROUGH THE READING OF THIS BOOK. JUST KNOW YOU HAVE A PURPOSE AND THE BEST WAY TO FIND THAT PURPOSE IS THROUGH GOD WHO LOVES YOU SO MUCH AND WANTS THE BEST FOR YOUR LIFE. IT MAY SEEM LIKE HE DOESN'T BECAUSE HE ALLOWS US TO MESS UP. +

WELL HE DID THAT FOR A REASON. REMEMBER GOD DIDN'T INTEND FOR HIS CHILDREN(US) TO BE HELD CAPTIVE UNLESS IT WAS TO GET US TO COME TO HIM OR COME BACK TO HIM. THE BEST WAY NOT TO BE HELD CAPTIVE AGAIN. IS BY MAKING GOD THE HEAD OF OUR LIVES. NO MATTER WHAT YOU'VE DONE, PEOPLE YOU'VE HURT AND HURTS TO YOURSELF.
GOD HAS A PLAN FOR YOUR LIFE.

TRY GOD AND WATCH HOW GREAT YOUR LIFE WILL BECOME. YOU HAVE NOTHING TO LOOSE........

CHAPTER 1

DAY 1
(Romans 11:36)
For from him and through him and to him are all things. To him be glory forever. Amen.

TODAY STARTS MY LAST 30 DAYS OF INCARCERATION COUNTDOWN. NOW I'M A SHORT TIMER. I MUST SAY THAT I'M NERVOUS. BUT ACCORDING TO THIS SCRIPTURE, GOD IS IN CONTROL. I KNOW THAT'S TRUE BUT I'M HUMAN AND I'M STILL WORRIED ABOUT MY FUTURE.

I JUST DON'T WANNA END BACK UP IN HERE. I STARTED FASTING TODAY, THE FIRST TWO WEEKS I WILL NOT BE EATING BREAKFAST, THEN IN THE 3RD WEEK NO BREAKFAST AND LUNCH. 4TH WEEK NO BREAKFAST, LUNCH BUT ON THE LAST DAY I'LL EAT NOTHING AT ALL.

I FEEL I HAVE TO DO THIS IN ORDER TO GET MY BODY AND MIND UNDER CONTROL. THIS WILL BE A MAJOR WAY OF DOING SO AND REAPING THE REWARDS FROM GOD ACCORDING TO MATT:6:17-18 SAYS:

17 But when you fast, anoint your head and wash your face, 18 that your fasting may not be seen by others but by your Father who is in secret. And your Father who sees in secret will reward you.

I HOPE TO DO A FAST AT LEASE ONCE A WEEK FOR THE REST OF MY LIFE. I JUST DON'T WANT MY PAST ANYMORE. TODAY HAS STARTED OUT OK, THANK GOD FOR WAKING ME UP TODAY. I'M A LAUNDRY TRUSTEE. THIS HELPS MY TIME GO BY FAST IN WHICH I

LIKE VERY MUCH. I THINK TOO MUCH. I'M ALWAYS BATTLING THINGS IN MY MIND, LIKE WHAT MY FUTURE HOLDS IN STORE FOR ME AFTER I LEAVE HERE. I JUST HAVE TO STOP WORRYING AND LET GOD GUIDE ME THROUGH.

I'M TO MEET WITH COMMUNITY CORRECTIONS SOON TO SET UP MY RELEASE TO REHAB, WHICH WILL BE THE NEXT PHASE OF MY LIFE. I WILL BE ON 3 YEARS PROBATION. COUNTY LOVES TO LOCK YOU UP FOR ANY KIND OF VIOLATION. WITH GODS HELP, I PLAN ON DOING ALL MY PROBATION IN STEPS. DO COMMUNITY SERVICE THEN TETHER,

FINES AND COST. I'M GONNA DO A.A. FOR THE REST OF MY LIFE. I'M POWERLESS OVER MY ADDICTION. ONCE GOD DELIVERS ME FROM MY ADDICTION, WHICH WILL KILL A AWFUL LOT OF MY PROBLEMS.

WOW!!!!! JUST SEEN 2 INMATES LEAVE FOR REHAB, IT'S AWESOME SEEING THAT. THAT LETS ME KNOW PEOPLE DO LEAVE HERE(JAIL)FOR REHAB AND GO HOME. AN INMATE SAID SOMETHING TO ME I DIDN'T LIKE, I'M LEARNING I CAN'T REACT TO EVERYTHING PEOPLE SAY TO ME. IF IT DON'T MATTER TOMORROW FORGET IT ABOUT AND MOVE ON. GOD IS REALLY WORKING WITH ME IN THIS AREA OF MY LIFE. MY LOW SELF-ESTEEM ALLOWS THINGS LIKE THAT TO BOTHER ME WHEN IT SHOULDN'T.

GOTTA STAY FOCUS ON GOD, THEN THINGS WILL WORK OUT. I CAN'T PLEASE EVERYBODY, I'M GONNA STOP TRYING. BEING A LAUNDRY TRUSTEE, I'M ABLE TO BLESS INMATES WITH UNDERWEAR AND OTHER CLOTHING. I CAN MAKE

SOMETHING OFF THE MANY THINGS I ACQUIRE AND I DO IF I KNOW THE PERSON HAS MONEY ON HIS BOOKS AND BEING BLESSED BY FAMILY AND OTHERS.

SINCE I'M BLESSED I CAN NOW BE A BLESSING.

THANK GOD. THE OTHER LAUNDRY TRUSTEE I WORK WITH JUST FOUND OUT HE HAS TO DO MORE TIME THAN HE THOUGHT. HE IS VERY CRUSHED. HE DON'T BELIEVE IN GOD, SO I CAN'T SAY IT WAS IS FOR A REASON. WELL LORD THANK YOU FOR BLESSING ME WITH THIS DAY. THANK YOU FOR LOVING ME ENOUGH TO LET ME KEEP MY HEALTH AND STRENGTH. THANKING YOU IN A ADVANCE FOR LETTING ME SEE TOMORROW.

DAY 2

(Acts 4:13)
Now when they saw the boldness of Peter and John, and perceived that they were unlearned and ignorant men, they marveled; and they took knowledge of them, that they had been with Jesus.

LORD I THANK YOU FOR BLESSING ME TO SEE ANOTHER DAY. I KNOW IT WAS YOU WHO WOKE ME TODAY. SO I THANK YOU. I'M LEARNING AND SEEING THE MORE I PRAY AND MEDITATE ON YOUR WORD, IT'S MAKING ME NOT AFRAID TO TALK ABOUT YOU PLUS IT'S HELPING ME IN OTHER AREAS OF MY LIFE. THANK YOU FOR SLOWLY TRANSFORMING ME.

ONLY YOU CAN DO THIS FOR ME. LAST NIGHT THE EX-GIRLFRIEND CAME TO MY MIND. I DO HOPE ONE DAY I CAN APOLOGIZE TO HER ALONG WITH MANY OTHER PEOPLE I HAVE HURT WITH MY ADDICTION, THIS IS PART OF MY RECOVERY (STEP 9 IN A.A & N.A): MADE DIRECT AMENDS TO SUCH PEOPLE WHEREVER POSSIBLE, EXCEPT WHEN TO DO SO WOULD INJURE THEM OR OTHERS. THIS HELP KEEP ME FROM COMING BACK TO JAIL. I REALLY WANT A CHANGE IN MY LIFE. I BELIEVE

ONCE PEOPLE SEE HOW GOD HAS CHANGED MY LIFE. THEY'LL BELIEVE THERE IS SOME KIND OF HIGHER POWER OUT THERE.

GOT A SHOWER THIS MORNING AFTER THANKING GOD FOR ANOTHER DAY. WONDER WHAT TODAY IS GOING TO BRING. MY BUNK MATE/CO-WORKER IS READING A BOOK THAT IS NOT GOING TO HELP HIM AT ALL PLUS HE'S CHEWING TOBACCO WHICH IS AGAINST JAIL RULES. I TRY TALKING TO HIM, IT SERVES NO PURPOSE.

HE KNOWS HE'S OVERWEIGHT AND ALL HE DOE'S IS PRETTY MUCH EAT A LOT, HE SAYS HE'S GOING TO START WORKING OUT WHILE IN HERE (JAIL) BUT HE SAYS A LOT OF THINGS BUT DON'T DO ANY OF THEM. IT REALLY BOTHERS ME WHEN PEOPLE SAY THEY GONNA DO SOMETHING THEN DON'T DO WHAT THEY SAID THEY WAS GOING TO DO.

I'M GLAD GOD IS A PERSON OF HIS WORD. THATS MY BUNK MATES LIFE. HE'S DOES KNOW A LOT ABOUT GOD AND THE BIBLE. HE SHOWED ME HOW TO USE THE BOOK OF PROVERBS. HE SHOWED ME PROVERBS HAS 31 CHAPTERS. FOR EVERY DATE OF THE CURRENT MONTH READ THE WHOLE CHAPTER THAT MATCHES THAT DATE OF THE MONTH. WOW YOU WILL BE SO SURPRISE WHAT YOU WILL LEARN BY READING IT THAT WAY. GOD CAN USE ALL KINDS OF PEOPLE AND THINGS TO TEACH AND SHOW YOU THINGS.

SO FAR TODAY HAS BEEN GOOD. MY OTHER LAUNDRY CO-WORKER IS SLOWLY COMING TO GRIPS WITH HIM STAYING HERE(JAIL) A LITTLE LONGER THAN HE FIGURED. I WISH HE BELIEVED IN THE BIBLE. I HOPE THAT CHANGES CAUSE HE HAS A VERY NEGATIVE OUT LOOK ON LIFE AND GOD. ONLY GOD CAN CHANGE HIS MIND. FOR ME IT'S A MUST TO CHANGE THE WAY MY MIND OPERATES ROMANS 12:2 SAYS:

DO NOT CONFORM TO THE PATTERN OF THIS WORLD, BUT BE TRANSFORMED BY THE RENEWING OF YOUR MIND. THEN YOU WILL BE ABLE TO TEST AND APPROVE WHAT GOD'S WILL IS--HIS GOOD, PLEASING AND PERFECT WILL.

IT'S HARD LISTENING TO THE RADIO, HEARING ABOUT THINGS THAT HAPPENS BY WHERE I LIVE. IT TOUCHES MY HEART BIGTIME. I NEED TO REMEMBER THIS WHOLE EXPERIENCE AND NEVER FORGET IT. WHAT A LEARNING EXPERIENCE THIS HAS BEEN. AS I GET CLOSER TO MY RELEASE DATE FROM HERE(JAIL). FEAR COMES OVER ME. I JUST HAVE TO REMEMBER WHAT THE WORD FEAR STANDS FOR: FALSE EVIDENCE APPEARING REAL.

ALL I NEED IS FAITH, HEBREWS 11:1 SAYS:
Now faith is the substance of things hoped for, the evidence of things not seen.

IT'S KIND OF A STRUGGLE FOR ME TO DO BUT GOD IS NOT THROUGH WITH ME YET. I WILL GET IT EVEN IF IT IS SLOW GO BUT I'LL GET THERE PHILLIPPIANS 3:14 SAYS:

I press on toward the goal to win the prize for which God has called me heavenward in Christ Jesus. I've wondered why I'm the way I am, makes me feel abnormal. How I can't be like other people(normal people).Why do I have so many demons, character defects, relationship issues, trust issues and inferiority complex. These problems and others only God can help me overcome 1 John 4:4 says: You, dear children, are from God and have overcome them, because the one who is in you is greater than the one who is in the world.

Me fasting and praying, I see it's working a lot of these problems out. I see my future getting better, thanks to God. Hebrews 11:40 says:
God having provided some better thing for us, that they without us should not be made perfect.

THIS WAS A BLESSED DAY THAT THE LORD MADE FOR ME, I'LL REJOICE AND BE GLAD IN IT. PHILIPPIANS 4:4 SAYS:

Rejoice in the Lord always. I will say it again: Rejoice!

I PRAY I SEE ANOTHER BLESS DAY LIKE TODAY BUT IF I DON'T I PRAY I'M IN HEAVEN WITH THE HEAVENLY FATHER 1 PETER 1:4 SAYS:

and into an inheritance that can never perish, spoil or fade. This inheritance is kept in heaven for you, All these blessings i ask in Jesus name thank god amen.

DAY 3

(John 14:15-17)

If ye love me, keep my commandments. And I will pray the Father, and he shall give you another Comforter, that he may abide with you for ever; Even the Spirit of truth; whom the world cannot receive, because it seethe him not, neither knoweth him: but ye know him; for he dwelleth with you, and shall be in you.

LORD THANK YOU FOR LETTING ME WAKE UP THIS MORNING. LAST NIGHT THE JAIL DEPUTY PLAYED THE RADIO IN OUR POD. A SONG BY NEW EDITION CAME ON NAME CAN YOU STAND THE RAIN. WHAT MEMORIES THAT SONG BROUGHT BACK TO ME. AT THE TIME WHEN THAT SONG WAS A HIT, I WAS GETTING OVER MY FIRST LOVE. BUT TIME HEALS ALL WOUNDS. PLUS THAT IS THE PAST BUT I STILL HAVE TO MAKE AMENDS TO THAT PERSON AS A PART OF MY HEALING PROCESS. THE MAIN THING I WANT IS GOD'S HOLY SPIRIT TO GUIDE MY LIFE; GALATIANS 5:16-26 SAYS:

I say then: Walk in the Spirit, and you shall not fulfill the lust of the flesh. 17 For the flesh lusts against the Spirit, and the Spirit against the flesh; and these are contrary to one another, so that you do not do the things that you wish. 18 But if you are led by the Spirit, you are not under the law.

19 Now the works of the flesh are evident, which are: adultery,[a] fornication, uncleanness, lewdness, 20 idolatry, sorcery, hatred, contentions, jealousies, outbursts of wrath, selfish ambitions, dissensions, heresies, 21 envy, murders,[b] drunkenness, revelries, and the like; of which I tell you before hand, just as I also told you in time past, that those who practice such things will not inherit the kingdom of

God.

22 But the fruit of the Spirit is love, joy, peace, long suffering, kindness, goodness, faithfulness, 23 gentleness, self-control. Against such there is no law. 24 And those who are Christ's have crucified the flesh with its passions and desires. 25 If we live in the Spirit, let us also walk in the Spirit. 26 Let us not become conceited, provoking one one another.

I WANT SO BAD TO BE A TOOL FOR GOD TO BLESS OTHERS, SO HE(GOD) WILL GET THE PRAISE AND THE GLORY. WELL BACK IN THE LAUNDRY ROOM WATCHING THE MACHINES GO ROUND AND ROUND. MY BUNK MATE/CO-WORKER IS SLEEPING AS USUAL. GOD IS HELPING ME GET MY MIND, BODY AND TONGUE UNDER CONTROL. WITH GOD IN CONTROL I CAN'T LOOSE, EVEN WHEN I'M TEMPTED GOD WILL MAKE A WAY OF ESCAPE FOR ME ACCORDING TO 1CORINTHIANS 10:13:

There hath no temptation taken you but such as is common to man: but God is faithful, who will not suffer you to be tempted above that ye are able; but will with the temptation also make a way to escape, that ye may be able to bear it.

SINCE MY PAST IS SOOOOOOOOOO BAD. I KNOW PEOPLE ARE GOING TO BE WATCHING FOR ME TO MESS UP AGAIN. IN WHICH THEY HAVE EVERY RIGHT TO THINK THAT. I CAN'T WORRY WHAT PEOPLE THINK OF ME BECAUSE THEY ONLY SEE THE OUTSIDE, THEY DON'T KNOW THE INSIDE OF ME ACCORDING 1SAMUEL 16:7:

But the Lord said unto Samuel, Look not on his countenance, or on the height of his stature; because I have refused him: for the Lord seethe not as man seethe; for man looketh on the outward appearance, but the Lord looketh on the heart.

SO WHEN IF AND WHEN I DO SLIP AGAIN BECAUSE I'M A HUMAN BORN INTO SIN. I KNOW GOD WILL FORGIVE ME, WHERE AS MAN TEND NOT TO FORGIVE AND LOOK DOWN ON YOU. THERE IS A SONG BY MARVIN SAPP CALLED THE BEST IN ME. WHAT A AWESOME SONG. WHEN PEOPLE START LOOKING DOWN ON YOU PLEASE LISTEN TO THIS SONG. I ALSO KNOW GODS LOVES ME NO MATTER MY FAULTS EVEN MORE THAN A MOTHER CAN LOVE HER CHILD.(THAT'S DEEP).

MY OTHER LAUNDRY/CO-WORKER JUST FOUND OUT HE'LL HAVE A PLACE TO GO TO AFTER HE LEAVES HERE(JAIL). A GUY HE HELP OUT YEARS AGO IS GOING TO LOOK OUT FOR HIM WHEN HE GET RELEASE FROM JAIL. HE DON'T BELIEVE IN THE GOD THING BUT HE DOES BELIEVE IN KARMA, WHAT GOES AROUND COMES BACK AROUND. I CALL IT GOD BECAUSE HAD PUT SERVICE IN OUR HEARTS BEFORE WE KNEW THE WORD KARMA MATT 7:12 SAYS:

Therefore all things whatsoever ye would that men should do to you, do ye even so to them: for this is the law and the prophets.

This just adds to my beliefs in God. Last night I came across a saying that's in a book I was reading. It said if a persons T.V. is bigger than their bookshelf, in most cases you can't trust that person. So I put it to the test by asking my

co-worker/bunk-mate. How big is his TV. He said 70 inches, then I ask him how big is his bookshelf, he said he didn't have one cause he don't read many if any books at all. The funny thing is I tell him all the time I can't trust him at all, because he's a back stabber. But there are a lot of people I know who don't read hardly at all that I can trust.

I believe the moral of this story is knowledge is power. Talked to the ex today, I'm glad she's still talking to me, she is also putting money on my books.

WOW A OLD SAYING COMES TO MY MIND THAT SAYS KILL THEM WITH KINDNESS, SHE'S KILLING ME. THE GLORY STILL GOES TO GOD BECAUSE HE'S TOUCHING HER HEART. THE LAUNDRY MACHINES MALFUNCTION TODAY, SO WE HAD A SHORT DAY IN LAUNDRY TODAY. I'LL REST, PRAY ALONG WITH READING. LORD I THANK YOU FOR ANOTHER BLESSED DAY YOU GAVE ME. I PRAY FOR MANY MORE DAYS LIKE TODAY WHICH WONT HAPPEN. BUT I KNOW THE LORD WILL GIVE THE STRENGTH TO ENDURE.

DAY 4

(2 Timothy 4:18)

The Lord will rescue me from every evil deed and bring me safely into his heavenly kingdom. To him be the glory forever and ever. Amen.

Another blessing today. God allowed me to see another day. I'm sure the enemy will be attacking me today with something, like he always do. With God on my side I'll be delivered from anything the enemy brings my way. Got a letter today form my case worker, stating she will be meeting with me in about 3 weeks to setup my release to rehab. That will be the next step in my journey.

I also got a business card from the jail chaplin, I'm hoping to meet up with other jail chaplains in jails and prisons on how we all can help inmates. This will be one of my ways of helping others. Most of all it will bring God glory. When I'm done with jail and rehab, I really wont have a place to go. Which will be a first in my

LIFE, I'LL BE LYING IF I SAY I DON'T HAVE FEAR AND BE AFRAID, I KNOW I'M SUPPOSE TO TRUST IN GOD BUT I'M HUMAN, SO THOSE THINGS DO COME INTO MY MIND. JESUS WAS AFRAID WHEN HE HAD TO FACE WHAT HE WAS UP AGAINST (MATTHEW 26:39 SAYS):

And going a little farther he fell on his face and prayed, saying, "My Father, if it be possible, let this cup pass from me; nevertheless, not as I will, but as your will.

WHAT I'M GOING TO GO THROUGH DON'T COMPARE TO WHAT JESUS WENT THROUGH. ON TOP OF IT ALL HE MADE IT THROUGH, SO I KNOW I CAN GET THROUGH THIS. TO THINK HE DIED FOR US(WOW). TO BE HONEST I'M NOT GOING TO DO THAT. ME AND MY BUNK-MATE /CO-WORKER WAS TALKING TODAY. I TOLD HIM ABOUT MY WRONGS I DID IN THE PAST IN WHICH I'M NOT PROUD OF. I THINK ABOUT THEM A LOT. I KNOW CERTAIN PEOPLE WILL NEVER FORGIVE ME. AS PART OF MY RECOVERY I HAVE TO MAKE AMENDS TO THEM ALL(STEP9). WELL THE EXHAUST ALARM WENT OFF AND SHUT DOWN THE DRYERS. THAT MAKES FOR AN EARLY DAY WHICH IS ALRIGHT WITH ME, I'M TIRED

Anyway, so much till I'm at the point to where I don't feel like writing how the day was. It's not about me, this is all for Gods glory after reading Matthew 25:14-30:

14 "Again, it will be like a man going on a journey, who called his servants and entrusted his property to them.

15 To one he gave five talents of money, to another two talents, and to another one talent, each according to his ability. Then he went on his journey.

16 The man who had received the five talents went at once and put his money to work and gained five more.

17 So also, the one with the two talents gained two more.

18 But the man who had received the one talent went off, dug a hole in the ground and hid his master's money.

19 "After a long time the master of those servants returned and settled accounts with them.

20 The man who had received the five talents brought the other five. 'Master,' he said, 'you entrusted me with five talents. See, I have gained five more.'

21 "His master replied, 'Well done, good and faithful servant! You have been faithful with a few things; I will put you in charge of many things. Come and share your master's happiness!'

22 "The man with the two talents also came. 'Master,' he said, 'you entrusted me with two talents; see, I have gained two more.'

23 "His master replied, 'Well done, good and faithful servant! You have been faithful with a few things; I will put you in charge of many things. Come and share your master's happiness!'

24 "Then the man who had received the one talent came. 'Master,' he said, 'I knew that you are a hard man, harvesting where you have not sown and gathering where you have not scattered seed.

25 So I was afraid and went out and hid your talent in the ground. See, here is what belongs to you.'

26 "His master replied, 'You wicked, lazy servant! So you knew that I harvest where I have not sown and gather where I have not scattered seed?

27 Well then, you should have put my money on deposit with the bankers, so that when I returned I would have received it back with interest.

28 " 'Take the talent from him and give it to the one who has the ten talents.

29 For everyone who has will be given more, and he will have an abundance. Whoever does not have, even what he has will be taken from him.

30 And throw that worthless servant outside, into the darkness, where there will be weeping and gnashing of teeth.'

IF I DON'T USE WHAT GOD HAS BLESSED ME WITH, IT CAN BE TAKEN FROM ME. I SO WANNA DO GODS WORK. I BELIEVE IT WILL BE BENEFICIAL FOR OTHERS AND MYSELF. BUT MORE FOR GODS KINGDOM, WHICH IS MORE IMPORTANT OVER EVERYTHING I COULD EVER WANT. WELL LORD I THANK YOU FOR A BLESSED DAY. IF IT WAS NOT FOR YOU, I WOULDN'T HAVE SEEN THIS DAY. THANK YOU AND I LOVE YOU.

DAY 5

(1 John 4:19)

We love him, because he first loved us.

(1 John 3:1)

Behold, what manner of love the Father hath bestowed upon us, that we should be called the sons of God: therefore the world knoweth us not, because it knew him not.

Another day in the land of the living, thanks to GOD. He really loves and forgives me when it's hard for me to love and forgive myself along with others.

Mark 11:25:
And when you stand praying, if you hold anything against anyone, forgive them, so that your Father in heaven may forgive you your sins.

THERE ARE 2 THINGS YOU CANT SLOW OR STOP. ONE IS TIME, TWO IS THE AGING PROCESS. TIME IS MOVING RIGHT ALONG WHICH MEANS I'M GETTING CLOSE TO MY RELEASE DATE FROM HERE(JAIL).

WHILE I'M AGING IN HERE, I'M GAINING MUCH KNOWLEDGE THROUGH READING GOD'S WORD(BIBLE) ALONG WITH BOOKS PURPOSE DRIVEN LIFE AND KEYS TO

YOUR EXPECTED END. IT'S SCARY GOD'S KNOWS EVERYTHING I DO (HEBREWS 4:12-13):
FOR THE WORD OF GOD IS ALIVE AND ACTIVE. SHARPER THAN ANY DOUBLE-EDGED SWORD, IT PENETRATES EVEN TO
DIVIDING SOUL AND SPIRIT, JOINTS AND MARROW; IT JUDGES THE THOUGHTS AND ATTITUDES OF THE HEART.

NOTHING IN ALL CREATION IS HIDDEN FROM GOD'S SIGHT. EVERYTHING IS UNCOVERED AND LAID BARE BEFORE THE EYES OF
HIM TO WHOM WE MUST GIVE ACCOUNT. IF I'M DOING OR TRYING TO DO THE RIGHT THINGS, I'M OK. GOD LOOKS AT THE HEART(1SAMUEL16:7):

But the LORD said to Samuel, "Do not consider his appearance or his height, for I have rejected him. The LORD does not look at the things people look at. People look at the outward appearance, but the LORD looks at the heart.

TWO OF US ARE WORKING TODAY, CAUSE IT'S SATURDAY AND IT'S SLOW ON SATURDAYS. WE ROTATE SATURDAY'S OFF EXCEPT ME, I WORK THEM ALL TO KEEP MY TIME GOING. THERE HAVE BEEN THINGS COMING TO MY MIND WHICH BOTHERS ME TO MY STOMACH. I WISH I COULD

JUST MOVE ON AND NOTHING BOTHER'S ME. SOME OF THE THINGS THAT BOTHERS ME HAVE NO IMPORTANCE AT ALL. I'M SITTING HERE READING AND TALKING TO MY BUNK-MATE(CO-WORKING). IT'S KINDA HARD TALKING TO HIM ABOUT A LOT OF THINGS BECAUSE OF THE AGE GAP. I'VE GOT TO LEARN HOW TO COMMUNICATE WITH PEOPLE OF ALL AGES, IF I PLAN ON HELPING OTHERS LIKE ME WITH ADDICTION PROBLEMS LIKE MYSELF. MY BUNK-MATE(CO-WORKER) MAKES IT HARD FOR ME TO LOVE HIM BUT I'M GOING TO(1 JOHN 4:7-12):

Beloved, let us love one another: for love is of God; and every one that loveth is born of God, and knoweth God.

8 He that loveth not knoweth not God; for God is love.

9 In this was manifested the love of God toward us, because that God sent his only begotten Son into the world, that we might live through him.

10 Herein is love, not that we loved God, but that he loved us, and sent his Son to be the propitiation for
our sins.

11 Beloved, if God so loved us, we ought also to love one another.

12 No man hath seen God at any time. If we love one another, God dwelleth in us, and his love is perfected in us.

I KNOW FOR A FACT I'VE MADE IT HARD FOR PEOPLE TO LOVE ME. I'M GLAD GOD WILL NEVER STOP LOVING ME. WITH ONLY 2 OF US WORKING TODAY, WE GET EVEN MORE FOOD ON TOP OF

what we already get. God is keeping me strong with the
fasting. Just as I'm writing how God is keeping me strong the devil just said in my mind, I'm wasting my time this book is not going to help anything or anyone.

That just lets me know I'm doing the right thing, why else will the devil say that in my mind, it's because he can see the future which makes him afraid. Fasting is really helping me gain control over my body, it's also something I'm gonna have to do when I'm release from here(jail). Today is going well so far besides me and my bunk-mate(co-worker) talking about all my wrongs I've done to ex-wife and son. It makes me feel so bad and sad.

We agree people can forgive but don't forget. The devil attacks me saying how are you(myself) going to make it when no one wants you and no where to go. I just

Know as long as I have faith in God, I'll be fine (Hebrews 11:1):
Now faith is the substance of things hoped for, the evidence of things not seen. This is going to be life changing for me but for the good. The devil will try to change back to the old way of thinking and acting. With God I'm closing the door to my past and opening the door to a brighter future in Christ. After eating dinner my bunk-mate (coworker) got into a argument that almost led to a fight with our other co-worker. This other worker sure is bull headed, can't tell him anything.

That's people what can you do but pray for them. My bunk-mate/co-worker used something I told him, the teacher in the jail told me. She said after 5 days of being released from jail the mind goes back into the mindset it had before incarceration. That's the mindset that got them incarcerated in the first place.

WHAT HE WAS SAYING IF I CAN'T CONTROL MYSELF IN JAIL HOW WILL I BE ABLE TO CONTROL MYSELF WHEN I'M RELEASED FROM JAIL. THEN TO TOP IT OFF HE SAID THE FLESH IS WEAK. I BELIEVE GOD WAS USING HIM TO TECH ME A LESSON. THE SCRIPTURES HE IS REFERING TO ARE IN MATTHEW 26:41:

Watch and pray, that ye enter not into temptation: the spirit indeed is willing, but the flesh is weak.

I can't let myself fall victim to my flesh. I looked up the word victim, one of the meanings was DESTROYED. Wow that's exactly what the devil wants to do to me and others. Overall today it's been a good day. Lord I thank you.

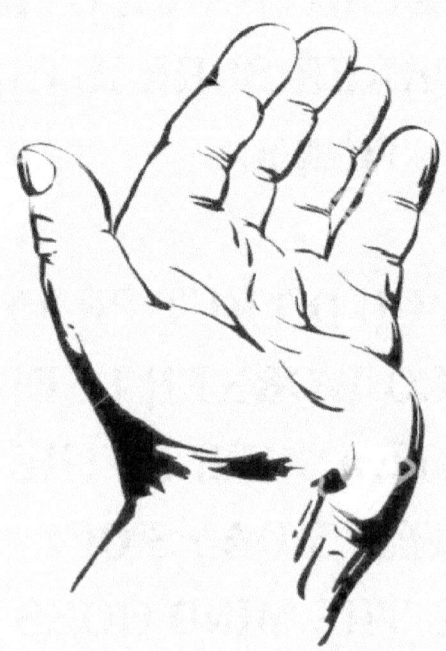

DAY 6

(James 1:13-15)

Let no one say when he is tempted, "I am being tempted by God," for God cannot be tempted with evil, and he himself tempts no one. 14 But each person is tempted when he is lured and enticed by his own desire. 15 Then desire when it has conceived gives birth to sin, and sin when it is fully grown brings forth death.

ANOTHER DAY THAT THE LORD ALLOWED ME TO SEE. LORD I THANK YOU FOR THIS DAY, IF IT WHERE NOT FOR YOU, I WOULD NOT BORE HERE. FUNNY CONVERSATION WITH BUNK-MATE/CO-WORKER ABOUT ME USING ALL HIS PENCILS, IN WHICH I USE TO DO MOST OF MY WRITINGS. I LIKE TO SAY THANK YOU S.B, FOR LETTING ME USE YOUR PENCILS. IN THE PROCESS OF US DEBATING ABOUT THE PENCILS, MY BUNKY ASK OUR OTHER COWORKER, WHO IS NOT FOND OF OUR RACE. IF HE COULD BORROW IS ERASER TO REMOVE A MISTAKE I MADE WHILE WRITING. HE SAID NO!!!!!!!!!!! I WISH YOU COULD SEE THE WAY HE SAID IT. HE HAS SAID IN SO MANY WAYS HE DON'T CARE FOR OUR RACE. WHICH IS VERY SAD BECAUSE GOD DON'T CARE WHAT RACE YOU ARE.
EPHESIANS 6:9 SAYS:

9 And, ye masters, do the same things unto them, for bearing threatening: knowing that your Master also is in heaven; neither is there respect of persons with him. We learn God doesn't look at color or race. He looks at the
inside(the heart)

1 Samuel 16:7 says:
But the Lord said unto Samuel, Look not on his countenance, or on the height of his stature; because I have refused him: for the Lord seeth not as man seeth; for man looketh on the outward appearance, but the Lord looketh on the heart.

ONLY GOD CAN CHANGE THE WAY PEOPLE VIEW EACH OTHER BUT IT'S JUST SAD HOW SOME PEOPLE ARE AND THE WAY THEY THINK. I GOT BLESSED WITH TOO MUCH LUNCH TODAY JUST ONE THE PERKS FOR BEING A TRUSTEE THEN I HAD TOO MUCH DINNER, GOD JUST KEEPS BLESSING ME. TODAY IS GRANDPARENTS DAY. I'M NOT A GRANDPARENT. MAYBE ONE DAY I HOPE I'M A BETTER GRANDPARENT THAN I WAS AS A PARENT. THAT'S ONE OF MY FAILURES THAT BOTHERS ME. I CAN'T CHANGE THE PAST ONLY THE FUTURE. I THANK GOD FOR MY SON STILL TALKING TO ME IN SPITE THE THINGS I PUT HIM AND HIS MOM THROUGH. MY MOTHER WHO PASSED A FEW YEARS AGO, BIRTHDAY IS COMING UP IN TWO DAYS. EVEN THOUGH SHE MAY NOT HAVE RAISED ME THE RIGHT WAY, ACCORDING TO SOCIETY. PLUS I HAD

ISSUES ON HOW SHE RAISED ME. I REALLY LOVE AND MISS HER VERY MUCH, I NEED HER NOW. I REMEMBER SOMETHING SHE ALWAYS SAID TO ME. SHE SAID SHE WAS THE ONLY BLOOD FAMILY I HAVE BESIDES MY SON. SHE WAS RIGHT AND TO THINK SOMETIMES I WOULD TALK TO HER IN A BAD WAY PLUS TOOK HER FOR GRANTED. I NEVER REALLY SAID I LOVE YOU TO HER. SHE WENT TO HER GRAVE NOT KNOWING IF HER ONLY CHILD
LOVED HER. THAT REALLY KILLS ME. THATS NOT RIGHT, NO ONE SHOULD GO THROUGH THAT. I WONDER WHY IM THE WAY I AM. I SEEM TO HURT **PEOPLE ALONG WITH MYSELF.**

> Each year in prison takes 2 years off an individual's life expectancy.

DAY 7

James (1:2-4)

2 My brethren, count it all joy when ye fall into divers temptations; **3** Knowing this, that the trying of your faith worketh patience.
4 But let patience have her perfect work, that ye may be perfect and entire, wanting nothing

I'M IN THE LAND OF THE LIVING. THANK GOD. HE KEEPS ON BLESSING ME. THIS IS JUST TOO MUCH LOVE. I DO KNOW IF NO ONE ELSE LOVES ME, GOD LOVES ME. THAT'S ALL THAT MATTERS. EVERYDAY I'M IN HERE I GO THROUGH SOMETHING MENTALLY. GOD GIVE'S ME THE STRENGTH TO GET THROUGH IT. IT'S JUST ANOTHER DAY JAILING, SOME ARE GOOD AND SOME ARE BAD. I STAY TO MYSELF, THAT'S HOW I JAIL.

I STARTED BACK TO READING THE BOOK CALLED: <u>THE KEYS TO YOUR EXPECTED END</u>. THIS BOOK IS A MUST READ. WHEN I'M DONE READING THE 24 CHAPTERS ON THE 24 DAY, MAY JAIL TIME WILL BE DONE. OFF TO REHAB I GO. I JUST SEEN THE DEPUTY WHO HELPS INMATES WITH ISSUES THEY MAY HAVE. SHE IS ONE OF A

FEW DEPUTIES WHO TREAT YOU LIKE A HUMAN BEING, UNLIKE SOME OTHER DEPUTIES. ONE THING I'VE LEARNED IN JAIL IS EVERYBODY THAT GOES TO JAIL IS NOT A CRIMINAL BUT IS TREATED LIKE ONE. I TELL YOU THE DEVIL KNOWS WHAT AND HOW TO ATTACK ME. I KNOW I CAN STAND ON GODS WORD IN 1 CORINTHIANS 10:13:

13 There hath no temptation taken you but such as is common to man: but God is faithful, who will not suffer you to be tempted above that ye are able; but will with the temptation also make a way to escape, that ye may be able to bear it.

THAT BEING SAID, WITH GOD THERE'S NOTHING I CAN'T HANDLE. GOD MUST REALLY PREPARING ME FOR SOMETHING IN HIS KINGDOM. THAT'S WHY THE DEVIL KEEPS ATTACKING ME. MY BUNK MATE/CO-WORKER IS HAVING LAZY DAY TODAY. HE HAS PRETTY MUCH DONE NOTHING TODAY.

I ADMIT IT'S MAKING ME MAD BUT I SHOULD BE USE TO IT. IT'S HELPING IN SERVANT HOOD. THIS IS GOOD PRACTICE. THANK GOD FOR A BIG LUNCH TODAY. HE JUST KEEPS BLESSING ME. I HAD TO SEE WHAT SOCIETY LABELS PEOPLE AS REAL BAD CRIMINALS. IT'S AWAKE UP CALL FOR ME.

Where they are housed at is like a dog caged up in a yard far away from the house. I'm housed in a penthouse compared to them. Again I'm blessed. I'm learning it can always be worst got to remember that.

Tomorrow is my mothers birthday. Happy birthday mom I love you, wish you was here. Now I'm even fuller from dinner, I'll watch our pro football team tonight. They're on Monday football. Today was a pretty decent day. After watching the game kinda made me think of the outside world. Well time for bed Lord I thank you for this day. Goodnight.

DAY 8

(Titus 2:6-8)

6 Young men likewise exhort to be sober minded.

7 In all things shewing thyself a pattern of good works: in doctrine shewing uncorruptness, gravity, sincerity,

8 Sound speech, that cannot be condemned; that he that is of the contrary part may be ashamed, having no evil thing to say of you.

THANKING GOD FOR ANOTHER DAY. HAPPY BIRTHDAY MOM LOVE YOU, WISH YOU WAS HERE. IT'S A NEW DAY. IN READING THESE SCRIPTURES. I KNOW I HAVE TO BE A GOOD EXAMPLE FOR GOD, THAT'S MY MAIN GOAL IN LIFE. THAT BEING SAID, I WONDER WHAT THE DEVIL GONNA HIT ME WITH TODAY, IT'S ALWAYS SOMETHING, IT'S USUALLY PAIN, WORRY OR TEMPTATION IN WHICH GOD MAKE A WAY OF ESCAPE(1CORITHIANS10:13):

13 There hath no temptation taken you but such as is common to man: but God is faithful, who will not suffer you to be tempted above that ye are able; but will with the temptation also make a way to escape, that ye may be able to bear it.

I'M COMING TO GRIPS WITH WHAT I'M FACING. TALK ABOUT BEING HUMBLED. I'M GONNA HAVE TO DEAL WITH THE WAY PEOPLE ARE GOING TO LOOK AT ME AND THE THINGS THEIR GOING TO SAY TO ME AND BEHIND MY BACK. I JUST GOTTA

REMAIN FOCUSED ON GOD. HE'S THE ONLY ONE GOING TO GIVE ME THE STRENGTH TO ENDURE. I CAN'T WAIT TO SIT DOWN IN THE FUTURE AND LOOK BACK ON ALL WHAT I JUST CAME THROUGH AND GOD ALL THE PRAISE. I'M SITTING HERE WATCHING THESE INMATES ROLL UP CIGARETTES WITH BIBLE PAPER(WTH). SOMETHING WRONG THERE.

BESIDES THAT, THIS DAY IS GOING GOOD. BEING A LAUNDRY TRUSTEE I GET SOME OF THE INMATES UNIFORMS WHEN THEY GO HOME OR REHAB. THAT LETS ME KNOW PEOPLE DO LEAVE JAIL WHEN THEIR TIME IS UP. PLUS MEANS MY DAYS ARE NUMBERED HERE. BUT WITH THE WAY MY MIND WORKS IT'S NEVER GONNA HAPPEN FOR ME. DEEP DOWN I KNOW IT IS. GOTTA PUT MY FAITH IN ACTION. I'M LEARNING IT'S BETTER TO FOCUS ON GOD, I GET FURTHER AND LESS STRESS. I READ IN ROMANS 15:4:

there is hope in my future and encouragement.

THE ONE THING I DON'T WORRY ABOUT IS FOOD IN HERE. I ATE GOOD FOR LUNCH AND DINNER. MY BUNK-MATE/CO-WORKER SAID HE CAN SEE THE DIFFERENCE IN ME. THANK GOD FOR THAT. THIS WAS NOT AN EVENTFUL DAY. TIME FOR BED. LORD I THANK YOU FOR THIS DAY.

DAY 9

(James 2:14)
What doth it profit, my brethren, if a man say he hath faith, but have not works? can that faith save him?

I'M AWAKE THANK GOD FOR BLESSING ME WITH ANOTHER DAY. I'M SURE THE ENEMY WILL BE ATTACKING MY FAITH. WHY TODAY WAS GOING GOOD THEN GOT BAD. I ALREADY HAVE TRUST ISSUES, THEN I COME TO JAIL AND THEY GET EVEN WORST. MY BUNK-MATE(CO-WORKER) PULLED A SCAM ON ME FOR HIS GAIN.

ALL I CAN SAY IS WOW.... I WAS MAD AT FIRST BUT HEY THIS IS JAIL, WHAT DO YOU EXPECT. MOST OF THE PEOPLE IN JAIL ARE UP TO NO GOOD. THEN 9 OUT OF THE 10 OF THEM ARE LYING. JAIL STANDS FOR: **JUST ANOTHER INMATE LYING**. I'M SURE THERE IS SOME UPSTANDING PEOPLE IN HERE. BUT I HAVE NOT MET THEM.

IT SEEMS LIKE EVERYBODY I PUT MY TRUST IN WHINES UP HURTING ME THIS GOES ALL THE WAY BACK TO MY CHILDHOOD. I JUST HAVE TO DO WHAT THE SCRIPTURE SAYS IN MICAH 7:5:

Trust ye not in a neighbor; put ye not confidence in a friend; keep the doors of thy mouth from her that lieth in thy bosom.

THIS WILL HELP ME GET BY. I DO KNOW I'M GONNA NEED TO TRUST SOMEONE. GOD WILL HAVE TO SHOW ME WHO I CAN TRUST. HAD A VERY INTERESTING CONVERSATION WITH ANOTHER INMATE, WE PICK AND JOKE WITH EACH OTHER ALL THE TIME. TODAY WE HAD A SERIOUS CONVERSATION ABOUT ME AND PEOPLE IN MY LIFE.

WHAT I'M I GONNA DO AFTER I'M RELEASED FROM JAIL AND REHAB AND THE PEOPLE I WILL KEEP IN MY LIFE. TO BE HONEST, I REALLY DON'T KNOW. I DO KNOW WHAT I WANT TO DO. IT'S WHATS WRITTEN IN JOHN 3:30:

He must increase, but I must decrease.

THIS WILL BE HARD FOR ME TO DO BECAUSE OF SELF. MY PRIDE IS GONNA WANT TO STEP IN, WHICH WILL CAUSE A MAJOR STRUGGLE FOR ME.

I READ IN RICK WARREN'S BOOK NAMED: **THE PURPOSE DRIVEN LIFE**. IT READS PRIDE BUILDS WALLS AND HUMILITY BUILDS BRIDGES. THIS IS SO TRUE. WHEN YOU'RE IN A SITUATION LIKE THIS (JAIL), YOU REALLY FIND OUT WHO'S GOT YOUR BACK.

THE ONE PERSON WHO SHOULD TELL ME WHERE TO GO, HAS HELPED ME SO MUCH IN THIS TIME OF NEED. THIS PERSON HAS EVERY RIGHT TO COMPLETELY WASH THEIR HANDS OF ME BUT HAS BEEN THERE FOR ME. THE ONE WHO SAID THEY LOVE ME HAS KICKED ME TO THE CURB.

IF YOU REALLY LOVE SOMEONE, NO MATTER WHAT THEY DO OR HAVE DONE TO YOU ARE STILL THERE FOR THAT PERSON. WHATEVER THEY HAVE DONE CAN BE WORKED OUT AND THROUGH WITH GOD'S HELP AND GUIDANCE. THAT LEADS

ME BACK TO A VERY TRUE SAYING. ACTIONS SPEAKS LOUDER THAN WORDS....... GOD'S ACTIONS SPEAKS LOUDER THAN WORDS, BY SENDING HIS ONLY SON TO DIE FOR OUR SINS JOHN 3:16:

For God so loved the world, that he gave his only begotten Son, that whosoever believeth on him should not perish, but have eternal life.

DON'T SAY IT IF YOU DON'T MEAN IT. MY LIFE HAS BEEN A MESS FOR SO LONG, PLUS I HURT, LET DOWN, AND SHAMED SO MANY PEOPLE. GOD'S WORD IN LUKE 3:5-6 SAYS:

5Every valley shall be filled, And every mountain and hill shall be brought low; And the crooked shall become straight, And the rough ways smooth.
6And all flesh shall see the salvation of God.

I believe in the process of God straightening my life out. I'll be able to use this situation in my life to help others Titus 3:14:
14And let our people also learn to maintain good works for necessary uses, that they be not unfruitful.

IT ALL STARTS WITH FAITH AND ME ACTING ON IT JAMES 2:26:

26For as the body apart from the spirit is dead, even so faith apart from works is dead.

I MUST SAY I'M REALLY LEARNING AND WILL TAKE A LOT FROM THIS EXPERIENCE. THE INMATE SAID SOMETHING THAT REALLY HIT ME VERY HARD. HE SAID HOW MANY PEOPLE THAT KNOW ME ARE SAYING I'M GONNA FAIL AGAIN.

I SAID A LOT OF THEM. BY ME KNOWING WHAT PEOPLE ARE THINKING, I HAVE TO STAND ON THE WORD IN ROMANS 8:31:
31What then shall we say to these things? If God is for us, who is against us.

I TOTALLY UNDER STAND WHY PEOPLE AND LOVE ONE'S FEEL THIS WAY ABOUT ME. IT'S BECAUSE OF THE THINGS I DID IN MY PAST. I WOULD FEEL AND SAY THE SAME ABOUT SOMEONE WHO DONE THE THINGS I'VE DONE. BUT THEY ARE NOT GOD OR HAVE A MIND OF GOD,

THANK GOODNESS FOR THAT. ACCORDING TO ROMANS 8:28:
28And we know that to them that love God all things work together for good, even to them that are called according to his purpose.

I'LL BE FINE. SO LORD I'M THANKING YOU IN ADVANCE. LORD I LOVE YOU AND THANK YOU FOR ANOTHER DAY.

DAY 10

(John 16:33)

These things have I spoken unto you, that in me ye may have peace. In the world ye have tribulation: but be of good cheer; I have overcome the world.

I'M UP AGAIN, THANK GOD. THE ENEMY (DEVIL) IS STARTING THE DAY OFF BY ATTACKING ME ABOUT MY FUTURE, ACCORDING TO JOHN 16:33:

Since jesus overcame the world. I can overcome world also.

TODAY IS 911. I REMEMBER IT LIKE IT WAS YESTERDAY AND WHERE I WAS AT WHEN THE PLANES HIT THE TOWERS. I WASN'T IN JAIL THEN, I HAD HOUSE, CAR, CLOTHES AND MONEY IN MY POCKET WHEN THAT HAPPEN.

WELL BACK TO THE MATTER AT HAND NOW. I WISH GOD HAD GOT MY ATTENTION IN A DIFFERENT WAY.

I NOW KNOW THIS WAS THE ONLY WAY HE COULD GET MY ATTENTION AS WRITTEN IN THE BOOK NAMED THE KEY TO YOUR EXPECTED END BY KATIE SOUZA. ME BEING HARD HEADED, MAKES

ME THINK OF THE OLD SAYING, A HARD HEAD MAKES A SOFT BEHIND, WELL MY BEHIND IS SOFT. WELL I'M STILL DOING MY FAST WITH GOD HELPING ME WITH IT. THAT'S WHY THE DEVIL IS ATTACKING ME THE WAY HE IS. HE KNOWS I DONT WANT MY OLD LIFE(COLOSSIANS 3:10): AND HAVE PUT ON THE NEW MAN, THAT IS BEING RENEWED UNTO KNOWLEDGE AFTER THE IMAGE OF HIM THAT CREATED HIM.

TODAY IS CHRISTMAS IN HERE(JAIL), IT'S COMMISSARY IN HERE. THERE WILL BE A LOT OF WHEELING AND DEALING AROUND HERE TODAY. THIS GIVES YOU THE TASTE OF THE OUTSIDE WORLD. TONIGHT THE FOOTBALL GAME IS ON. THE STEELERS AND RAVENS ARE PLAYING.

THIS IS ALSO THE GAME WITH THE TEAM THAT CANCELED A PLAYERS CONTRACT AND SUSPENDED HIM FROM THE NFL. I AM REALLY BECOMING A SHORT TIMER. HOW WILL I REACTED WHEN I LEAVE HERE?

I KNOW FOR SURE I'LL BE DOING WHAT GODS WORD SAYS ACCORDING TO 1 THESSALONIANS 5:16-18:

16 Rejoice always;
17 pray without ceasing;
18 in everything give thanks: for this is the will of God in Christ Jesus to you-ward.

MY BUNK-MATE/CO-WORKER OF MINE IS REALLY GETTING TO ME. THIS HAS TO BE A TEST I KEEP FAILING. I JUST DON'T LIKE BEING AROUND PEOPLE I KNOW IS STRAIGHT UP BACK STABBING ME AND UP TO NO GOOD, HE'S GOOD FOR SAYING WHAT A PERSON WANTS TO HEAR BY SAYING HE'S GOING TO DO SOMETHING AND KNOWING ALL ALONG HE'S NOT GOING TO.

THIS FAST I'M ON IS REALLY HELPING ME DEAL WITH HIM AND LIFE IN JAIL. TODAY I OVER HEARD A DEPUTY TALKING TO AN INMATE WHO RETURNED FROM COURT. THE DEPUTY ASK THE INMATE HOW DID COURT GO TODAY? THE INMATE REPLIED THE PROSECUTOR IS OFFERING 20 YEARS. THE DEPUTY TOLD HIM HE BETTER TAKE THAT OFFER.

Wow that would destroy me. It's hard enough doing these months. This made me realize if I go back to my old ways and not let God lead my path, I can be facing the same situation or even worst. Well back to my pod my bunk-mate had a nice cook up you think he offered me any? Nope!!!!!!!

I said to him I give you my whole breakfast and lunch tray plus do other things for you, even with you scamming me. He said I should have asked, I said I shouldn't have to ask. I'll use this as a learning lesson for serving others.

I read in Habakkuk 1:5:

Behold ye among the nations, and look, and wonder marvellously; for I am working a work in your days, which ye will not believe though it be told you.

This lets me know I'll be surround by great things I can't believe. It all leads back to, all things works together for the good of them who love the Lord.

I'm tired and want to relax then sleep. Oh yea another day down. Thank God.

DAY 11

(Psalms 126:1-6)

When Jehovah brought back those that returned to Zion, We were like unto them that dream. **2** Then was our mouth filled with laughter, And our tongue with singing: Then said they among the nations, Jehovah hath done great things for them. **3** Jehovah hath done great things for us, Whereof we are glad. **4** Turn again our captivity, O Jehovah, As the streams in the South. **5** They that sow in tears shall reap in joy. **6** He that goeth forth and weepeth, bearing seed for sowing, Shall doubtless come again with joy, bringing his sheaves with him.

DANG I'M UP AGAIN. THIS SHOWS ME HOW MUCH GOD LOVES ME. EVEN THOUGH I'M IN HERE(JAIL). THIS IS STILL A JOYFUL DAY, SO I CAN HAVE J.O.Y IN WHICH I READ IN A BIBLE. J STANDS FOR JESUS, O STANDS FOR OTHERS, Y STANDS FOR YOURSELF.

WHAT I GET OUT OF THIS IS LET JESUS LEAD YOUR LIFE WHILE YOU HELPING OTHERS ,IN RETURN YOURSELF WILL BE BLESSED. LAST NIGHT WAS ONE OF THOSE CRAZY EMOTIONS HIT ME.

WHY DO I THINK AND WORRY SO MUCH? WORRYING CAN KILL A PERSON,THESE ARE WAYS THE DEVIL CAN TARE A PERSON DOWN AND KILL THEM. I GOTTA

GET MY FAITH UP, BECAUSE THERE IS NO WORRY IN FOLLOWING JESUS. I'M SLOWLY GETTING MY MIND WRAP AROUND THAT, ROMANS 8:5 SAYS:

For they that are after the flesh mind the things of the flesh; but they that are after the Spirit the things of the Spirit.

THIS MORNING I LEARNED A LESSON. I WAS COMPLAINING TO MY BUNK-MATE/COWORKER ABOUT HIMSELF. WELL THERE IS 2 SIDES TO EVERY STORY. I DECIDED TO TELL HIM MORE ABOUT HIMSELF, IN WHICH I CALLED HIM A BACKSTABBER AND OTHER THINGS. HE GOT TIRED OF EVERYTHING BEING SO ONE SIDED, SO HE LET ME HAVE IT ABOUT MYSELF. OH WOW HOW HUMBLING WAS THAT. MATTHEW 23:12 SAYS:

And whosoever shall exalt himself shall be humbled; and whosoever shall humble himself shall be exalted.

I ACTUALLY COULDN'T SAY A WORD. HE WAS SO RIGHT ABOUT THE THINGS HE SAID ABOUT ME. HE SURE LET THE WIND OUT OF MY SAIL. 1CORINTHINS 4:6 SAYS:

Now these things, brethren, I have in a figure transferred to myself and Apollos for your sakes; that in us ye might learn not to go beyond the things which are written; that no one of you be puffed up for the one against the other.

THIS HIT REALLY HIT HOME. I CAN NEVER EVER THINK OF MYSELF ABOVE ANOTHER PERSON.

JESUS DIDN'T DO THAT WHEN HE REALLY COULD, PHILIPPIANS 2:5-8 SAYS:

Have this mind in you, which was also in Christ Jesus:
6 who, existing in the form of God, counted not the being on an equality with God a thing to be grasped,
7 but emptied himself, taking the form of a servant, being made in the likeness of men; **8** and being found in fashion as a man, he humbled himself, becoming obedient even unto death, yea, the death of the cross.

I GOT TO REMEMBER PRIDE BUILDS WALLS WHILE HUMILITY BUILDS BRIDGES. IF I BUILD A WALL OF PRIDE, I CAN'T HELP PERSON ACROSS THE BRIDGE TO GOD. THE ONLY PRIDE I SHOULD HAVE IS IN GOD PHILLIPPIANS 3:3 SAYS:

for we are the circumcision, who worship by the Spirit of God, and glory in Christ Jesus, and have no confidence in the flesh.

LORD I THANK YOU I REALLY NEEDED THIS(ROMANS 8:28):

28And we know that to them that love God all things work together for good, even to them that are called according to his purpose.

THE OTHER LAUNDRY TRUSTEE I WORK WITH, CAN'T TELL HIM TO MUCH OF ANYTHING. VERY BULL HEADED. HE REALLY DON'T WANT TO HEAR ANYTHING ABOUT GOD. I DO BELIEVE ONE DAY HE WILL REALIZE HE NEEDS GOD IN HIS LIFE. TODAY WAS A VERY UNEVENTFUL DAY BUT A VERY BLESS ONE. LORD I THANK YOU FOR ANOTHER DAY.

DAY 12

(Romans 15:13)
Now the God of hope fill you with all joy and peace in believing, that ye may abound in hope, in the power of the Holy Spirit.

BLESSED WHAT MORE CAN I SAY. IF I'M WRITING THIS I'M BLESSED TO BE ABLE TO WRITE TODAYS EVENTS CAUSE GOD WOKE ME TODAY. TODAY IS THE DAY MY LAUNDRY CO-WORKER IS OFF, HIS ROTATION FOR HIS OFF DAY IS TODAY. MYSELF AND MY COWORKER/BUNK-MATE WILL HAVE A GOOD DAY ANYWAY.

IT'S A SLOW GO SO FAR. WE ONLY HAVE TO WASH THE LAUNDRY FROM ONE FLOOR TODAY. SO I'M ABLE TO CATCH UP ON READING. I REALLY ENJOY READING RICK WARREN'S BOOK THE PURPOSE DRIVEN LIFE(WWW.PURPOSEDRIVENLIFE.COM), KATIE SOUZA THE KEY TO YOU EXPECTED END(WWW.EXPECTEDENDMINITRIES.COM). MY FAVORITE BOOK IS THE BIBLE, IT'S WHERE I READ IN EPHESIANS 4:22-24:

That ye put away, as concerning your former manner of life, the old man, that waxeth corrupt after the lusts of deceit; **23** *and that ye be renewed in the spirit of your mind,* **24** *and put on the new* *man, that after God hath been created in righteousness and holiness of truth*

This is what it will take for me to stay on the right path for my purpose. It's not going to be easy because I've lived a certain way for so long. I know I must not give up. God is preparing me so I don't give up when I get on the outside. This way it wont be any surprises I can't handle. On our way to the floor with the laundry will have to wash.

We walked down this one hallway where the evidence room is located. There must have been a drug bust last night, the hallway smelled like marijuana. This smell was so strong it gave me a headache, my bunk-mate/co-worker loved that smell, took him forever to stop talking about it. He sure do love his weed, he lights up like a light bulb when he talks about. If he can talk about weed like that, surely I can talk about God the same way when given the opportunity

SPECIALLY AFTER ALL HE'S DONE FOR ME.
(EPHESIANS 1:3):
Blessed be the God and Father of our Lord Jesus Christ, who hath blessed us with every spiritual blessing in the heavenly places in Christ

I CAN'T FORGET THIS JAIL EXPERIENCE OR MY PAST BUT I DON'T WANT IT IN MY FUTURE. IF I ALLOW MY PAST INTO MY FUTURE, I'LL GET WHAT I'M RECEIVING IN MY PRESENT(JAIL,MISERY). I'M AT A MAJOR FORK IN THE ROAD FOR MY LIFE. WHILE THE LAUNDRY WAS WASHING MY BUNK-MATE/CO-WORKER AND MYSELF GOT INTO A LONG CONVERSATION ABOUT MY MOTHER, WHICH IS ONE OF MY BIGGEST REGRETS IN MY LIFE.

SHE PASSED NEVER KNOWING IF I LOVED HER. HE STILL HAS HIS MOTHER BUT THEY HAVE ISSUES WITH EACH OTHER. I TOLD HIM TO FIX WHATEVER PROBLEMS THEY BECAUSE YOU ONLY HAVE ONE MOTHER. WHEN SHE'S GONE YOU'LL NEVER GET THAT BACK AND YOU DON'T REGRET LIKE I HAVE, THE REGRET I HAVE IS CAUSING ME A LOT OF PAIN. NEXT WEEK IS GOING TO BE EVEN MORE

FASTING, I REALLY WONT TO GET MY FLESH UNDER CONTROL(MATTHEW 26:11):

Watch and pray, that ye enter not into temptation: the spirit indeed is willing, but the flesh is weak.

FOR GOD TO USE ME, MY FLESH CAN'T TAKE OVER. NOTHING GOOD WILL COME OF THAT IF THAT HAPPENS. IT WILL MOST LIKELY BE DEATH, THEN THE ENEMY HAS WON.

I RATHER BE A WINNER WITH GOD. THE ENEMY IS ATTACKING ME NOW, HE'S TELLING ME THE THINGS I'M GONNA GO THROUGH AND HOW ROUGH IT WILL BE FOR ME TO DO WHAT I WANT TO DO FOR CHRIST. HE KNOWS MY WEAKNESSES IN WHICH HE'S TRYING TO USE THEM AGAINST ME(1 PETER 5:8):

Be sober, be watchful: your adversary the devil, as a roaring lion, walketh about, seeking whom he may devour.

ALL THIS TELLS ME I'M DOING SOMETHING RIGHT FOR GOD. I'M NOT ONLY GOING TO BE BLESSED, I'M GOING TO BE A BLESSING WHICH WILL HELP LEAD PEOPLE TO GODS KINGDOM. WHICH IS THE ULTIMATE GOAL.

Well my bunk-mate/co-worker used me again for his gain, I'm not even mad, he did ask first before he used me. God is slowly working with me. Lord I thank you for another blessed day.

DAY 13

(Romans 3:23-24)

For all have sinned, and fall short of the glory of God; **24** being justified freely by his grace through the redemption that is in Christ Jesus.

Well my my the Lord allowed me to see another day. Thank you Lord. According to these scriptures, I have to take blame for all mess ups and mistakes. I learned in here a mistake is when you don't know the outcome.

To be honest, I pretty much knew the outcome if I kept doing what I was doing. I'm not in jail because of a mistake. It's because of my own doing.

We all are giving choices of right and wrong, Matthew 6:24 says:

No man can serve two masters; for either he will hate the one, and love the other; or else he will hold to one, and despise the other. Ye cannot serve God and mammon.

Today all three of us are back to work. Today is trustee laundry day. Each one of us have our own personal inmate who we do extra for them, such as bleach and

FOLDING OF CLOTHES. WE GET PAID WITH COMMISSARY, MY BUNK-MATE/CO-WORKER GETS PAID OTHER THINGS I PREFER NOT TO MENTION. BEING A TRUSTEE HAS MANY PERKS. WE ALWAYS COME ACROSS THINGS LIKE T-SHIRTS, SOCKS, FOOTES, LONG JOHNS TOP&BOTTOM WHICH CAN BE ALL SOLD FOR EVEN MORE COMMISSARY. IT'S KIND OF BUSY DOING OUR PREFERRED INMATES THEN THE REGULAR INMATES. THE ENEMY IS AT IT AGAIN,

I'LL JUST HAVE TO IGNORE HIM AGAIN. HE'S REALLY SEEING I DON'T WANT THAT OLD WAY OF LIVING ROMANS 8:13 SAYS:

for if ye live after the flesh, ye must die; but if by the Spirit ye put to death the deeds of the body, ye shall live.

I'M LIVING A BLESSED LIFE EVEN IN JAIL. IT ALL STARTED WHEN I DECIDED TO PUT GOD FIRST IN MY LIFE(MATTHEW 6:33):

But seek ye first his kingdom, and his righteousness; and all these things shall be added unto you.

I READ IN A FAMOUS BOOK THAT SAID, WHAT WE COMMITTEE OURSELVES TO NOW IS WHAT WE BECOME LATER IN LIFE. SO IF I FOLLOW CHRIST

now and study his word. My life will become a loving, caring and a blessing to others all the while leading people to gods kingdom. As of today I have 17 days till I'm release to rehab. One of my favorite Prince songs is 17 Days. Everyday I say a little prayer asking God to help me trust him. I tend to mess up when I do things my way(Proverbs 3:5):

Trust in Jehovah with all thy heart, And lean not upon thine own understanding.

You don't have gratitude till you've had pain, in which will cause you to change but some people still won't change even after pain. Today is ending on a good note, my son and ex-wife came to see me today. I was hoping they came to see me before left here(jail).

My ex has moved on. I was not good for her, I really wish her the best. Well as Ice Cube would say today was a good day. Thank God.

DAY 14

(Philippians 4:6)
Do not be anxious about anything, but in everything by prayer and supplication with thanksgiving let your requests be made known to God.

THERE'S A SAYING I'VE HEARD MANY TIMES. IT SAYS I'M TOO BLESS TO BE STRESS. I'M BLESS TO SEE ANOTHER DAY. MY NO BREAKFAST AND LUNCH STARTS TODAY.

I GOT TO FOCUS ON MYSELF THROUGH GOD HELPING ME. THE FIRST TEST WILL BE TURNING BACK THE BREAKFAST AND LUNCH TRAYS. THIS WILL HELP GET MY MIND AND BODY UNDER CONTROL EVEN MORE. IT'S ALREADY WORKING, MY BUNKMATE/CO-WORKER KINDA MADE ME MAD BY SOMETHING HE DID BUT I DIDN'T FLY OFF THE HANDLE, I JUST SHOOK MY HEAD AND KEPT GOING,THANK GOD FOR THAT(EPHESIANS 4:26).
Be angry and do not sin; do not let the sun go down on your anger.

EVERYTHING I NEED TO KNOW IS IN GODS WORD,THE BIBLE. I WAS TOLD IN HERE THE WORD BIBLE MEANS:B-BASIC,I INFORMATION, B-BEFORE,L-LEAVING,E-EARTH, WHEN YOU THINK

ABOUT THAT IS THE TRUE MEANING OF THE BIBLE (2 TIMOTHY 3:16).

All Scripture is breathed out by God and profitable for teaching, for reproof, for correction, and for training in righteousness.

I JUST READ IN ONE OF MY INSPIRATIONAL BOOKS WHERE IT TOLD AN EASTERN MONARCH, WHO HAD A LOT OF WORRIES ALL AROUND HIM. HE GATHERED ALL HIS SMARTEST MEN TOGETHER. HE TOLD THEM TO COME UP WITH A MOTTO THIS IS SHORT, SWEET AND WILL HELP IN ANY SITUATION.

THEY THOUGHT FOR A WHILE AND CAME WIH THE SAYING. THIS TO SHALL PASS AWAY (WOW). IN OTHER WORDS NOTHING LAST FOREVER ALSO IF THINGS ARE GOING GOOD OR BAD JUST WAIT IT WILL CHANGE. THIS LETS ME KNOW THAT WHEREVER I'M AT IN THE PRESENT TIME OF MY LIFE JUST WAIT IT WILL CHANGE.

LAST NIGHT I HAD AN INMATE SAY TO ME, DO I KNOW HOW MANY PEOPLE WHO HAVE BEEN INCARCERATED HAVE WRITTEN BOOKS ABOUT

JAIL & PRISON. LETTING ME KNOW I'M NOT THE FIRST TO WRITE A BOOK ABOUT INCARCERATION. HE'S RIGHT BUT I LOOKED AT THAT STATEMENT AS AN ATTACK OF THE DEVIL TRYING TO DISCOURAGE ME.

I JUST HAVE TO RESIST HIS ATTACKS WITH GODS HELP(JAMES 4:7):

Submit yourselves therefore to God. Resist the devil, and he will flee from you.

THE SAME INMATE ASK ME TO WRITE A LETTER FOR HIM TO HIS JUDGE ASKING SENTENCE REDUCTION. I WROTE THE LETTER WHILE I WAS AT WORK IN THE LAUNDRY ROOM. WHEN I BROUGHT THE LETTER TO HIM TO GO OVER IT WITH HIM, HE TOLD ME TO WAIT BECAUSE HE IS WATCHING TV(WOW).

I'M HELPING HIM AND HE TELLS ME TO WAIT, THAT'S JUST PEOPLE. JUST HAVE TO CHAULK IT UP AS A LESSON LEARNED(PSALMS 118:8).

It is better to take refuge in the Lord than to trust in man.

HAD A CONVERSATION TODAY, TALKING ABOUT HOW INMATES GET RELEASED FROM incarceration and come right back in a few days. Most inmates are on probation when they are release from incarceration. So they have to report to their probation officer the next day after release from incarceration. When they report to their probation officer, they fail the drug test.

How is that possible when they was just release the day before. It's because they was still getting hi while being incarcerated and went straight from incarceration to drug house to celebrate being release from incarceration. On average once inmate is release from incarceration he or she is back incarcerated within 3 months.

The main reason for this is the inmate is going back to the same environment that cause he or she to be incarcerated. This make it very very very hard for the

INDIVIDUAL TO DO THE RIGHT THING ALONG WITH LOW SELF-ESTEEM AND VOIDS IN THEIR LIFE. I HAVE BOTH. I'VE DONE MANY THINGS TO DEAL WITH THESE ISSUES, I KNOW AND KNEW GOD IS THE ONLY ONE WHO CAN HELP ME WITH THESE ISSUES, BUT I STILL MADE BAD CHOICES. THIS TIME I'M GOING TO USE GOD TO HELP ME WITH MY MANY ISSUES (PSALMS 145:19).

He fulfills the desire of those who fear him, he also hears their cry and saves them.

I REALLY DON'T KNOW HOW I'M GOING TO MAKE IT AFTER INCARCERATION AND REHAB. I WILL HAVE NOTHING, NO WHERE TO GO, NO JOB, NO WIFE, DIFFICULT PROBATION, SELF PITY, TALK DOWN TO, SHAMED, THAT'S A LOT FOR A OLDER PERSON LIKE MYSELF TO HANDLE.

I THINK ABOUT THIS EVERYDAY AND IT REALLY HURTS BAD BUT EVERY-TIME I THINK ABOUT ALL THIS, A LITTLE VOICE IN MY HEAD SAYS IT'S GONNA BE OK, BECAUSE HAVE FAITH AND GODS WORD (HEBREWS 11:6).

And without faith it is impossible to please him, for whoever would draw near to God must believe that he exists and that he rewards those who seek him.

Another day down. I'm still happy to have seen my son and ex-wife the other day. That means a lot to me, just knowing somebody took the time to come see me. The best way to show someone you care is give them your time.

These have been the only people who has always had my back and been there for me. I will never forget all they've done for me. I know God is going to make it where I can show my appreciation. Lord thank you for blessing me **TODAY.**

DAY 15

(Colossians 3:2)
Set your mind on the things that are above, not on the things that are upon the earth.

CAN YOU BELIEVE THIS? GOD WOKE ME TO SEE ANOTHER DAY, THIS JUST LETS ME KNOW HOW MUCH HE LOVES ME. LIKE THE SCRIPTURE SAYS, I HAVE TO FOCUS ON THINGS ABOVE. THIS WILL BE VERY HARD FOR ME TO DO BUT I AM MAKING PROGRESS THANKS TO MY HIGHER POWER(GOD). TODAY IS MY BUNK-MATE/CO-WORKER BIRTHDAY. HE SAID HE'S NOT WORKING MUCH TODAY. WHAT I DON'T UNDERSTAND IS THAT HE DOES THAT ANYWAY(LOL). MY EX-WIFE AND SON PUT MONEY ON MY BOOKS FOR MY LAST 2 WEEKS HERE. I READ IN A CHRISTIAN BOOK LAST NIGHT, THAT SAID GET RID OF THINGS THAT REMINDS ME OF THE OLD LIFE. IN 2 CORINTHIANS 5:17 SAYS THE SAME:

Wherefore if any man is in Christ, he is a new creature: the old things are passed away; behold, they are become new.

I DON'T HAVE A LOT OF MATERIAL REMINDERS TO GET RID OF. THE THINGS I REMEMBER, I'VE DONE TO MYSELF AND OTHERS WILL BE VERY HARD

FOR ME TO GET RID OF. FOR MY ME TO CHANGE FROM MY OLD LIFE WILL TAKE SOME TIME, I DIDN'T GET THIS WAY OVERNIGHT. AS LONG AS I FOCUS ON GOD, I WILL SLOWLY CHANGE FROM MY OLD WAY OF THINKING(MATTHEW 6:33):

But seek ye first his kingdom, and his righteousness; and all these things shall be added unto you.

I KNOW WHEN THE ENEMY ATTACKS ME WITH CERTAIN THINGS FROM MY PAST AND SAYING I CAN'T ACHIEVE CERTAIN THINGS I WAT TO ACHIEVE. THAT'S A SIGN FOR ME I'M ON THE RIGHT TRACK.

THE ENEMY DOESN'T WANT THIS, SO HE'LL ANYTHING HE CAN TO DISCOURAGE ME BECAUSE HE DOESN'T WANT ME TO HELP IN GOD'S KINGDOM. BUT WHEN I'M ATTACKED, I KNOW GOD WILL MAKE AWAY OF ESCAPE(1 CORINTHIANS10:13):

There hath no temptation taken you but such as man can bear: but God is faithful, who will not suffer you to be tempted above that ye are able; but will with the temptation make also the way of escape, that ye may be able to endure it.

God has guidelines for us to follow, that will help in the change in our life a lot easier(2 Corinthians 1:13):

For we write no other things unto you, than what ye read or even acknowledge, and I hope ye will acknowledge unto the end.

SURRENDERING TO GOD MEANS WE'LL HAVE TO CHANGE THE WAY A PERSON THINKS AND HIS OR her lifestyle which can lead to fear. The best definition I heard for the word fear is false evidence appearing real.

I was talking to my bunk-mate/co-worker about fear, which I related to an experience I had in elementary school. I was one of the tough kids in 6th grade. One day a 4th grader made me mad, I told him I was going to beat him up after school. When I went to beat him up, he was so afraid(fear) of me, till when I approached him, he started swinging his arms like a windmill at me(like a girl), I couldn't get a punch in at all. He even made slip and fall, all the kids laugh at me and I lost my tough kid reputation that day. I stayed away from every since that day(lol). It's getting close to me being released to rehab.

After that is what I'm afraid(fear)of. I'm about to take on a fight that looks like I

CAN WIN. BUT I'M GONNA HAVE GOD ON MY SIDE PLUS I'M GONNA BE SWINGING LIKE A WINDMILL TO KNOCK THE ENEMY DOWN WHICH WILL MAKE HIM THINK TWICE ABOUT ATTACKING ME. THE JAIL HAD A DEATH TODAY. HE WAS IN HIS 50'S, I HEAR HE CHANGED COLORS AND WHIND UP DYING. I HOPE HE KNEW CHRIST AS HIS SAVIOR. (ROMANS 8:13):

For if ye live after the flesh, ye must die; but if by the Spirit ye put to death the deeds of the body, ye shall live.

HE MAKES THE 3RD PERSON TO DIE SINCE I BEEN HERE(JAIL). CLOSING IN ON THE END OF ANOTHER DAY. LORD I THANK YOU FOR BLESSING THROUGH ANOTHER DAY.

Jail can be a blessing in disguise...

BIRTHDAY IN JAIL...

THIS IS MY FIRST AND LAST BIRTHDAY IN JAIL. IT REALLY IS ANOTHER DAY TO ME. AFTER A CERTAIN AGE ITS LETTING YOU KNOW HOW OLD YOU'RE GETTING. THEY ARE BLESSINGS BECAUSE YOU SEE ANOTHER BIRTHDAY. I'VE BEEN BLESSED TO SEE MANY OF THEM. LORD I THANK YOU EVEN IF I AM IN JAIL.

MY EX-WIFE SENT ME A HAPPY BIRTHDAY CARD. I KNOW GOD HAD TO BE IN THAT BECAUSE SHE SHOULD BE TELLING ME WHERE TO GO. I'VE BEEN ABLE TO DO A LOT OF SOUL SEARCHING, I REALIZE THERE HAS TO BE A CHANGE IN MY THOUGHTS AND ACTIONS. FOR THAT TO HAPPEN IN ME GOD MUST COME FIRST IN MY LIFE. GOD IS GOING TO CHANGE THIS NEGATIVE INTO A POSITIVE IN MY LIFE. CAN'T WAIT TO SEE WHERE I WILL BE NEXT YEAR AT THIS TIME. STAY TUNED.

CHAPTER 2

DAY 16

(1 Corinthians 15:33)

Do not be deceived, bad company ruins good morals.

ANOTHER DAY IN THE LAND OF THE LIVING. THANK YOU LORD FOR BEING BLESSING ME TO SEE ANOTHER DAY. ACCORDING TO THIS SCRIPTURE, I CAN'T BE AROUND BAD COMPANY. IN HERE(JAIL), I HAVE NO CHOICE. CAN'T TRUST ANYONE, I CAN'T EVEN TRUST MY BUNK-MATE/CO-WORKER. HE IS ALWAYS UP TO SOMETHING, IT'S CALLED SHOOTING MOVES IN HERE(JAIL). HE'S ALWAYS
SHOOTING MOVES BEHIND MY BACK IN WHICH I ALWAYS COME UP ON THE SHORT END. IT DON'T BOTHER ME ANYMORE IT'S PREPARING ME FOR THE OUTSIDE WORLD(PSALMS 25:5):

Guide me in thy truth, and teach me; For thou art the God of my salvation; For thee do I wait all the day.

I'M ASKING GOD FOR THIS FOR THE REST OF MY LIFE. I FOR SURE CAN'T GUIDE MYSELF, A BLIND PERSON CAN SEE THAT. LAST NIGHT I WAS LOOKING AT MY BIN. I WAS SEEING AGAIN HOW BLESSED I AM. WHEN I GOT TO JAIL, I HAD ONE PAIR OF UNDERWEAR & SOCKS TO HAVING 10 PAIRS OF UNDERWEAR AND 9 PAIRS OF SOCKS,

THAT'S JUST WHAT I KEPT. I WAS SO BLESSED I GAVE AWAY A LOT TO OTHER INMATES. IT'S A AWESOME FEELING HELPING OTHERS. I WAS GOING TO GIVE MY BELONGINGS TO MY BUNKMATE/CO-WORKER AFTER I LEAVE HERE(JAIL), I TOLD HIM HE HAD TO PASS IT ON WHEN HE LEAVES. I CHANGED MY MIND BECAUSE OF ALL THE UNDERMINING THINGS HE'S DONE TO ME AND OTHERS. I REALLY DON'T SEE HIM PASSING THEM ON, TO BE A BLESSING TO SOMEONE ELSE. I JUST DON'T TRUST HIM. WE SUPPOSE TO LOOK OUT FOR EACH OTHER IN HERE SINCE WE BUNK- MATES BUT THAT DON'T HAPPEN, HE'S ALWAYS UP TO NO GO, LOOKING TO PULL A FAST ONE ON ME OR WHOMEVER HE CAN. I GUESS WHAT DO YOU EXPECT THIS IS JAIL. MOST EVERYONE IN HERE HAD DID SOMETHING WHERE THEY GOT OVER ON SOMEONE. I JUST GOT TO REMEMBER THE NUMBER 1 RULE IN HERE(JAIL), TRUST NO ONE IN HERE(JAIL). MY BUNK-MATE/
CO-WORKER LOST HIS STEP-BROTHER A COUPLE DAYS AGO, I WON'T SAY ANYTHING TILL HE

MENTION SOMETHING TO ME ABOUT HIS PASSING. RIGHT NOW HE'S CRYING. HIS STEP-BROTHER WAS A BAD ALCOHOLIC AND IS BELIEVED TO HAVE DIED IN HIS SLEEP. HOPE HE KNEW HIS MAKER BEFORE HE PASSED OR CALLED ON THE LORD(PSALMS 55:16):

As for me, I will call upon God; and the Lord shall save me.

TODAY IS A GOOD LUNCH TRAY. BUT I WANT GOD TO DO A WORK IN ME. SO I'LL GIVE IT AWAY(FASTING). THIS WILL HELP ME IN ALL AREAS OF MY LIFE, BY HELPING ME GAIN SELF DISCIPLINE. THE ENEMY(DEVIL) IS NOT GOING TO STOP ATTRACTING ME, HE WANTS TO DESTROY ME(1 PETER 5:8):

Be sober, be watchful: your adversary the devil, as a roaring lion, walketh about, seeking whom he may devour

IF THE ENEMY CAN'T GET ME ONE WAY HE'LL FIND OTHER WAYS. HE CAUSE ME TO GET SOOOOOOO MAD AT MY OTHER CO-WORKER TILL I PUT HANDS ON HIM AND WAS ABOUT TO HURT HIM. IF I DID THAT, I WOULD'VE LOST EVERYTHING, WOULDN'T BE ABLE TO LEAVE WHEN I'M SUPPOSE TO HERE(JAIL) PLUS IT

WOULD'VE BEEN ANOTHER CASE ON ME, WHICH WOULD'VE CAUSE ME TO HAVE MORE JAIL TIME. ON TOP OF ALL THAT I WOULD'VE BEEN PLACE WITH THE REAL BAD CRIMINALS. I DID ALL THIS WHILE FASTING, THIS WASN'T SUPPOSE TO HAPPEN. I FEEL TOTALLY DOWN. I WANNA GIVE UP, I FEEL LIKE A TOTAL FAILURE. THE ENEMY(DEVIL) IS REALLY ATTACKING ME NOW BUT I KNOW HE IS THE AUTHOR OF LIES. GOD HELP ME THROUGH THIS. LORD FORGIVE ME FOR ALL THE
WRONG I'VE DONE AND HELP ME TO GROW STRONGER SO THIS WON'T HAPPEN AGAIN. LORD I THANK YOU FOR FORGIVING ME. THE OLD ME ROSE UP IN ME, THAT LET'S ME KNOW, I GOT A LONG WAY TO GO. I REALLY THOUGHT I WAS DOING GOOD. GOD SHOWED ME I NEED TO FAST AND PRAY MORE THAN I'VE BEEN. THE ENEMY WON THIS BATTLE BUT HE WON'T WIN THE WAR(PSALMS 27:3):

Though a host should encamp against me, My heart shall not fear: Though war should rise against me, Even then will I be confident.

WITH THE LORD BEHIND ME, I WON'T FEAR

HIM(PSALMS 18:6-7):

In my distress I called upon Jehovah, And cried unto my God: He heard my voice out of his temple, And my cry before him came into his ears. Then the earth shook and trembled; The foundations also of the mountains quaked And were shaken, because he was worth.

I'll pick myself up, wipe the dirt off and be ready to get back into the battle. Outside of this ordeal, today is still a blessed day. I got paid pretty well today by the inmates for bleaching and folding their clothes.

I'M NOT GOING TO GIVE UP EVEN THOUGH THE ENEMY(DEVIL) WANTS ME TO BUT WE ALL FALL SHORT(JAMES 3:2):

For in many things we all stumble. If any stumbleth not in word, the same is a perfect man, able to bridle the whole body also.

IT'S NOT ABOUT FALLING DOWN BUT GETTING BACK UP(ROMANS 3:23-24):

For all have sinned, and fall short of the glory of God.

Being justified freely by his grace through the redemption that is in Christ Jesus. I told another inmate how much time I got left. He replied your journey begins. I said you're right. I don't know where this jouney is going to lead me. I have faith in God to know this journey will end for the glory of the Lord. I'm determined to stay on this path(Romans 3:22):

Even the righteousness of God through faith in Jesus Christ unto all them that believe; for there is no distinction.

LORD I THANK YOU FOR THE LESSON I LEARNED TODAY. THANK YOU FOR LOVING ME. LORD I LOVE YOU. I HOPE AND PRAY THAT I'M ALLOWED TO SEE ANOTHER DAY BUT IF NOT. I KNOW I'M COMING TO LIVE WITH YOU.

DAY 17

(Hebrews 11:6)

And without faith it is impossible to be well-pleasing unto him; for he that cometh to God must believe that he is, and that he is a rewarder of them that seek after him.

GOD IS GIVING ME ANOTHER CRACK AT IT. LORD I THANK YOU FOR THIS DAY. LAST NIGHT I WAS WOKEN UP TO MY BUNK-MATE/CO-WORKER USING THE BATHROOM, THEN FOR SOME REASON I GOT DEPRESSED. I DON'T KNOW WHY BUT THAT'S ME. THE LEFT SIDE OF MY CHEST IS BOTHERING ME, PROBABLY STRESS. I HATE I STRESS MYSELF OUT. MOSTLY ALL THE TIME I STRESS MYSELF FOR NO REASON, JUST ABOUT EVERYTHING I WORRY ABOUT ENDS UP WORKING OUT BETTER THAN I HOPED. I KNOW WHAT THIS SCRIPTURE SAYS TO DO. I JUST GOTTA HAVE FAITH. IT'S HARD FOR ME TO JUST HAVE FAITH BECAUSE THINGS AND PEOPLE HAVE FAILED ME SOOOOOO MUCH. AT THIS POINT IN MY LIFE ALL I HAVE IS FAITH SO I GOT TO PUT IT TO USE (HEBREWS 11:1):

Now faith is assurance of things hoped for, a conviction of things not seen.

I DO SEE IT WORKING. WELL TODAY IS CHRISTMAS IN THE JAIL. TODAY IS COMMISSARY DAY. GONNA SEE A WHOLE LOT OF DIFFERENT ATTITUDES AROUND HERE TODAY. THIS DAY GIVES THE FEELINGS OF BEING ON THE OUTSIDE. THERE'S GONNA BE A LOT OF WHEELING AND DEALING TODAY. I'M BLESSED TO BE A BLESSING TO OTHERS. I TURNED BACK MY LUNCH TRAY BUT I'M EATING SMALL AMOUNTS OF PEANUTS AND COOKIES, GOD DOESN'T WANT ME TO KILL MYSELF WHILE FASTING. THIS IS SOMETHING I NEED AND WANT TO DO IN ORDER TO GET MY FLESH UNDER CONTROL, THE FLESH CAN EASILY GET WEAK(MATTHEW 26:41):

Watch and pray, that ye enter not into temptation: the spirit indeed is willing, but the flesh is weak.

MY CO-WORKERS ARE ALSO LOVING ME BEING ON A FAST(LOL). IT'S MORE FOOD FOR THEM TO EAT. SO I'M BEING A BLESSING TO THEM. THIS FAITH THING IS WORKING, EVEN THOUGH I'M FACING SOME BIG OBSTACLES, THERE IS NOTHING BIGGER THAN MY GOD(ROMANS 8:31):

What shall we then say to these things? If God be for us, who can be against us.

So I'm learning to put these obstacles in their place, in other words they're not as big as they appear with God on your side. People and things still come to my mind, all I can say is actions speaks louder than words. What a true saying. Gods actions has been really speaking to me. What a life lesson this has been for me. Today is one of the trustees birthday he really didn't tell anybody cause it's in here(jail).

I wish him a happy birthday anyway. I also had my birthday in here(jail) in which the whole kitchen staff singed happy birthday to me, which was pretty cool. After a while your birthdays is just another day and don't mean much anymore. I do thank God for allowing me to see another year alive and healthy.

Today an inmate gave me a new bible of a different translation, that had to be God because I was just saying to myself I need a bible of a different translation. I just don't see how people can say there is no God, if a person just look around at the universe you can see there is a God.

I helped an inmate write a sentence reduction letter today, I'm getting a lot of practice at doing this. This is going to be one of my business in which I hope can help those incarcerated. It's a awesome feeling helping others.

Well as Ice Cube would say today was a good day. Lord I thank you for allowing me to have another day in the land of the living.

DAY 18

(Philippians 4:8)
Finally, brothers and sisters, whatever is true, whatever is noble, whatever is right, whatever is pure, whatever is lovely, whatever is admirable—if anything is excellent or praiseworthy—think about such things.

According to this scripture everything I need to think is all in God and the good things in my life. Lord I thank you for another day you have blessed me with again. Even with all my failures you still woke me. Next week I will be into the single digits to my release, which means I'm getting close to the next step of my journey.

I bet a pack of Raman noodles on the football game from last night in which I lost. The team I bet to win was loosing 28-0 in the first quarter. Oh well I'm blessed to have many packs of Raman noodles, loosing one is not going to hurt at all. In fact the night before I'm to be released I'm going to give pretty much all my food and clothing away. I'm not going to work

TO HARD TODAY AND JUST CHILL FOR A LIL BIT. (PHILIPIANS 1:6):

Being confident of this, that he who began a good work in you will carry it on to completion until the day of Christ Jesus.

SINCE I'M ABOUT TO EMBARK ON THIS NEW JOURNEY IN MY LIFE, ACCORDING TO THIS SCRIPTURE GOD IS GOING TO BEGIN A GOOD WORK IN ME. I'M REALLY HOPING THAT IS TRUE, IT IS SO IN MY HEART TO HELP OTHERS AND BRING ALL THE GLORY TO GOD.

I ALSO HOPE THE WORDS I SAY IN THESE WRITINGS ALONG WITH THE THE THINGS I PLAN ON DOING FOR GOD AND INMATES WILL BRING GLORY TO GODS KINGDOM. I DON'T WANT MY WILL ANYMORE, LOOK WHERE MY WILL HAS LANDED ME. I MUCH RATHER LET GODS WILL BE DONE(MATTHEW 6:10):

Your kingdom come, your will be done, on earth as it is in heaven.

I HAVE TO ADMIT WHEN I ATTENDED CHURCH AND DID GODLY THINGS, MY LIFE WAS PRETTY GOOD, MY LIFE WENT HEY WIRE WHEN I STARTED DOING MY OWN THING. SITTING HERE WITH THESE

MACHINES THINKING ABOUT MY PAST AND HOW I HAVE TO USE MY PAST TO CHANGE MY FUTURE. FOR SOME STRANGE REASON MY PALM KEEPS ITCHING, I'VE HEARD IT SAID WHEN THAT HAPPENS, I'M GOING TO COME INTO A LOT OF MONEY.

IT MUST BE A LOT OF MONEY BECAUSE IT SURE ITCHES A LOT. IF OR WHEN THAT DOES HAPPEN, I'M GOING TO GIVE GOD HIS PORTION(10%). I DON'T SEE WHY I CAN'T GIVE GOD HIS PORTION. I'VE PAID LAWYERS, PROBATION COST, COURT COST, TETHER COST, FINES AND COST, IMPOUND FEES, CAR RENTAL FEES, COMMUNITY SERVICE AND FEES FOR COMMUNITY SERVICE THEN MOST OF ALL JAIL TIME, WHICH IS TIME I CAN NEVER GET BACK.

IF I HAD FOLLOWED GOD AND HIS WORD. DO YOU KNOW HOW MUCH IT WOULD COST? 0 ZERO AND I WOULD BE SO BLESSED. BY GODS GRACE I CAN STILL LIVE A BLESSED LIFE. I GOTTA SIT MY PRIDE ASIDE AND HUMBLE MYSELF(JAMES 4:6):

But he gives us more grace. That is why Scripture says: God opposes the proud but shows favor to the humble.

MY BUNK-MATE/CO-WORKER IS AT IT AGAIN, SHOOTING MOVES THAT GET ME INVOLVED. I'LL BE SELLING HIM OUT. I TOLD HIM TO STOP DOING THAT BUT O WELL. TODAY'S LUNCH WAS GOOD TODAY BUT I PUSHED IT AWAY. I'M GETTING BETTER AT THAT THANK GOD, I'M SLOWLY CHANGING, I LOVE IT. THIS IS A CHANGE OF LIFE(COLOSSIANS 3:10):

And have put on the new man, which is renewed in knowledge after the image of him that created him.

CHANGE REQUIRES LOST OF OLD WAYS. IT'S GONNA BE HARD CHANGING MY OLD WAYS, I MUST ADMIT. BUT THERE'S NOTHING TO HARD FOR GOD. IT TOOK A WHILE FOR ME TO GET THIS WAY(HEBREWS 10:36):

For ye have need of patience, that, after ye have done the will of God, ye might receive the promise.

R.G.N.D.W.M. REMEMBER GODS NOT DONE WITH ME. TODAY IS SLOWLY COMING TO AN END, TOMORROW IS SATURDAY IN WHICH I HAVE TO WORK EVEN THOUGH IT'S SUPPOSE TO BE MY DAY OFF BUT I SOLD IT FOR 2 HONEY BUNS(LOL). SINCE I'VE BEEN A TRUSTEE, I'VE EVERY

Saturday in the jail. I have to work along with the other co-worker I had the confrontation with. I won't loose it again. I just got to put God first and I'll be fine.

Well Lord I thank you for this day you allow me to see. If I don't wake tomorrow, I thank you for my time on earth.

MY PET SPIDER

THERE WAS THIS SPIDER WHO HAD A WEB OUTSIDE MY WINDOW. HE ONLY CAME OUT AT NIGHT IN HOPES OF CATCHING INSECTS OR BUGS. I'VE WATCHED HIM WAIT IN THE MIDDLE OF THAT WEB FOR HOURS. SOME NIGHTS HE DIDN'T HAVE MUCH LUCK BUT HE DID GET LUCKY MORE OFTEN THAN NOT. HE STOOD STRONG IN THE MIDDLE OF THAT WEB, WITH THE WIND BLOWING LIKE CRAZY AND POURING DOWN RAIN. THIS WOULD CAUSE

HALF OF HIS WEB TO BE TORN OFF, THAT DID NOT STOP HIM FROM STANDING STRONG IN THE MIDDLE OF THAT WEB. I'M THINKING HE SHOULD RUN AND HIDE.

HE DIDN'T THINK THAT. HE STAYED IN THE MIDDLE OF THAT WEB AND STILL WAS ABLE TO FEED(WOW). ONE DAY THE WEATHER WAS REAL BAD, TO THE POINT IT WIPE OUT HIS WEB COMPLETELY OUT. I SAID TO MYSELF HE'S DONE AND DEAD. THREE DAYS HAD WENT BY AND NO SIGN OF HIM. ON THE FORTH DAY DURING THE NIGHT, THERE HE WAS BUILDING HIS WEB. WHEN HE WAS DONE HE WENT RIGHT BACK TO THE MIDDLE OF THE WEB STANDING STRONG. I LEARNED A LESSEN FROM THAT SPIDER. I LEARNED IF YOU WAIT AND BE PATIENT, GOOD THINGS WILL COME YOUR WAY EVENTUALLY. ALSO IF THE TROUBLES OF THE WORLD TARE YOU DOWN. PICK YOURSELF UP, REGROUP, WORK YOUR WAY BACK TO STAND STRONG. SOME WILL SAY THAT'S EASIER SAID THAN DONE. YES IT IS TRUE , YOU WILL NEED HELP GETTING BACK UP.

The good news is, there is someone who can help you like no other. That person is God. In studying his word, you'll learn patients, how to handle problems no matter what they may be. Along with that you'll live a blessed and fulfilling life that will also bless others. Just don't let the enemy win by making you give up. God loves you and he has your back.

You to can stand strong like my pet spider (1 Peter 1:6-7):

6 In this you rejoice greatly, even though now for a little while, if necessary, you have been distressed by various trials, 7 so that the genuineness of your faith, which is much more precious than gold which is perishable, even though tested and purified by fire, may be found to result in [your] praise and glory and honor at the revelation of Jesus Christ.

CHAPTER 3

DAY 19

(Matthew 7:12)
So in everything, do to others what you would have them do to you, for this sums up the Law and the Prophets.

IT'S HERE ANOTHER DAY I'M BLESSED WITH. LORD I THANK YOU FOR ALLOWING ME TO SEE ANOTHER DAY. THESE 2 LADIES IN COMMISSARY DON'T CARE FOR ME TOO MUCH BECAUSE OF A COMMENT I MADE WHILE JOKING WITH THE OTHER INMATES. NOW THEY SEE ME A CERTAIN WAY, IN OTHER WORDS THEY'RE JUDGING ME. THEY'VE TALK TO OTHER INMATES ABOUT ME, THE OTHER INMATES TRIED TELLING THEM I'M NOT LIKE THAT BUT THEY WASN'T HEARING IT.

THIS JUST MAKES ME REALIZE PEOPLE WILL ALWAYS JUDGE YOU KNOW MATTER WHAT, NOW THAT I'VE BEEN INCARCERATED, I'M REALLY GONNA BE JUDGED. IT DOESN'T HELP THAT MY PAST IS NOT THE BEST, PEOPLE ARE NOT GOING TO BELIEVE I'VE CHANGED. SAD PART OF ALL THIS, THEY CAN SEE I'VE CHANGED BUT THEY WILL STILL REFUSE TO ACCEPT IT. THEY STILL will look at me as that person I was in the past, there is nothing I can do about that. All I can do is move on from my past and give 1000% to not repeat my past. There will be people waiting for me to repeat my past so they can say I told you so or I knew it. I have a lot internal issues that only God and treatment can help.

Mostly all judges know you by whats on your case file and what the probation officer recommends. Judges can't take the time to get to know every offender, that's totally understandable. People also only know you by what you've done or have been told what you've done. When a person see or meet you, they've already formed an opinion(judgment) about you without out knowing you or
your past. That's life. But you know what ? God knows the heart(1 Samuel 16:7):

But the Lord said to Samuel, "Do not consider his appearance or his height, for I have rejected him. The Lord does not look at the things people look at. People look at the outward appearance, but the Lord looks at the heart.

It's two of us working today, which means even more food trays but you know what? I'm gonna push them away(discipline). Which I'm gonna need discipline and the strength to fight off my demons, along with temptations. Can't forget prayer(1 Thessalonians 5:17-18):

17 pray continually, **18** give thanks in all circumstances

THANK GOD ME AND MY OTHER CO-WORKER THAT I GOT INTO THE CONFRONTATION WITH A FEW DAYS WE'RE GETTING ALONG GREAT. ANY OTHER TIME I WOULD BE HOLDING A GARAGE AND NOT WANT TO WORK WITH HIM(ECCLESIASTES 7:9):

Do not be quickly provoked in your spirit, for anger resides in the lap of fools.

I KNOW I'M ON FIRE FOR THE LORD BECAUSE I'M INCARCERATED AND GOD IS ALL I GOT WHILE IN HERE, BUT WHAT ABOUT WHEN I GET BACK INTO SOCIETY? I'M PRAYING I DON'T PUT GOD ON THE BACK BURNER(ROMANS 12:11):

Never be lacking in zeal, but keep your spiritual fervor, serving the Lord.

IF I DO THAT, I WILL REVERT BACK TO THE OLD ME AND END BACK UP IN JAIL. I CAN'T FORGET WHO BROUGHT ME OUT. IN EVERYTHING I DO GOD HAS TO BE FIRST IN MY LIFE ALWAYS. I GOT TO RESIST THE DEVIL MY LIFE DEPENDS ON THIS(JAMES 4:7):

Submit yourselves, then, to God. Resist the devil, and he will flee from you.

I GOTTA STAY PRAYED UP, CAUSE THE DEVIL

HAS BEEN TRICKING PEOPLE FOR THOUSANDS OF YEARS, GOD IS THE ONLY ONE WHO CAN HELP ME FIGHT HIM(1 TIMOTHY 6:12):

Fight the good fight of the faith. Take hold of the eternal life to which you were called when you made your good confession in the presence of many witnesses.

I HAVE THE FAITH GOD WILL SEE ME THROUGH. TALK TO THE EX TODAY, SHE REALLY DON'T WANT ME BACK BUT I DON'T BLAME HER ONE BIT. I'M REALLY ON MY OWN WHEN I'M DONE WITH JAIL AND REHAB. BUT I'M NEVER ALONE WITH GOD ON MY SIDE. NO MATTER HOW BIG A PROBLEM MAY SEEM NONE IS BIGGER THAN GOD. GOD WILL NOT PUT MORE YOU THAN YOU CAN BARE(1 CORINTHIANS 10:13):

There hath no temptation taken hold of you but such as is common to man. But God is faithful; He will not suffer you to be tempted beyond that which ye are able to bear, but with the temptation will also make a way to escape, that ye may be able to bear it.

THE ENEMY JUST ATTACK ME SAYING I SHOULD STOP WRITING THIS BOOK CAUSE I HAVE OTHER THINGS TO WORRY ABOUT. SINCE HE'S ATTACKING ME I MUST BE DOING SOMETHING RIGHT. WE DON'T WALK BY SIGHT BUT BY FAITH(2 CORINTHIANS 5:7):

For we live by faith, not by sight.

I JUST READ THE WHOLE CHAPTER OF ECCLESIASTES. ALL I CAN SAY IS WOW!!!!!!!!!! IT'S DEEP. IT'S TIME FOR BED. LORD I THANK YOU FOR ANOTHER DAY.

DAY 20

(Ecclesiastes 9:11)

I returned, and saw under the sun, that the race is not to the swift, nor the battle to the strong, neither yet bread to the wise, nor yet riches to men of understanding, nor yet favour to men of skill; but time and chance happeneth to them all.

FIRST OF ALL I LIKE TO THANK GOD FOR BLESSING ME WITH ANOTHER DAY. I READ THIS SCRIPTURE LAST NIGHT RIGHT BEFORE BED, IT LETS ME KNOW LIFE ISN'T FAIR. SO EVERYTHING IN LIFE HAS A REASON AND A PURPOSE AND IT'S ALL FOR GOD'S GLORY. THE ENEMY(DEVIL) IS ALWAYS TEMPTING ME TO GIVE UP, BUT GOD HAS ME ROOTED IN HIS WORD, TILL I CAN'T GIVE UP. I KNOW WHAT THE FUTURE HOLDS FOR ME. THE DEVILS IS A THIEF AND A LIAR, I CAN'T LISTEN TO HIM, I ALSO READ ECCLESISATES 3:1-8:

To every thing there is a season, and a time to every purpose under the heaven:
2 A time to be born, and a time to die; a time to plant, and a time to pluck up that which is planted;
3 A time to kill, and a time to heal; a time to break down, and a time to build up;
4 A time to weep, and a time to laugh; a time to mourn, and a time to dance;
5 A time to cast away stones, and a time to gather stones together; a time to embrace, and a time to refrain from embracing;
6 A time to get, and a time to lose; a time to keep, and a time to cast away;
7 A time to rend, and a time to sew; a time to keep silence, and a time to speak;
8 A time to love, and a time to hate; a time of war, and a time of peace.

I'M LEARNING EVERYTHING HAS IT'S SEASONS(TIME). IT'S NOT HOW YOUR LIFE STARTS, IT'S HOW IT ENDS. TODAY IS TRUSTEE LAUNDRY DAY, WHICH MEANS I'LL RECEIVE EXTRA THINGS FOR BLEACHING AND FOLDING THEIR CLOTHES. NO MATTER HOW THE DAY ENDS, IT'S STILL GONNA BE A BLESSED AND GREAT DAY. I RECEIVED MAIL TODAY FORM MY SON. IT FEELS GOOD TO KNOW HE STILL LOVES ME. I CAN'T WAIT FOR US TO START BACK WORKING TOGETHER. A FIGHT BROKE OUT IN MY POD LAST NIGHT, WHICH WAS THE BIG TOPIC OF CONVERSATION TODAY.

NO LUNCH FOR ME TODAY, MY BODY IS SLOWLY GETTING USE TO THIS. THIS DAY IS MOVING RIGHT ALONG SMOOTHLY. JUST TAUGHT ABOUT HOW BAD MY EX-WIFE TALKED TO ME YESTERDAY. I'VE ALWAYS TOLD HER SHE DON'T KNOW HOW TO TALK TO PEOPLE, I REALLY SHOULD BE USE TO IT, BUT I SEE I'M NOT.

After I leave jail and rehab it's going to get even worst, cause all the pain I cause her. This is my final full week here(jail), am getting nervous as it gets closer and closer, I'm going to be more and more emotional. Today turned out to be an awesome day. When ever I hear from my son it's a awesome day. I didn't stress out to bad today, thank God. Well time to read the word, pray then sleep.

Lord I thank thank you again for another day in the land of the living.

DAY 21

(Isaiah 1:19-20)

If you are willing and obedient, you will eat the good things of the land; **20** *But if you resist and rebel, you will be devoured by the sword. For the mouth of the Lord has spoken.*

Yep here again. The Lord blessed me to see another day. Lord I thank you. In reading the word last night, in Isaiah if I don't obey, I'm doom to die. Wow! Deep. I don't believe it just means a physical death, a person can die a mental and spiritual death also. Besides finding NA/AA meetings to attend,

I want to find a church to fellowship at and grow spiritually and mentally and bless the church with the income God has allow me to have. By blessing Gods house, I'll be blessed in returned, not only in money but in all areas of my life. I blew so much money on unnecessary things. So why not give to God (John 10:28-29).

I give them eternal life, and they shall never perish no one will snatch them out of my hand. **29***My Father, who has given them to me, is greater than all no one can snatch them out of my Father's hand.*

TODAY IS GOING GOOD SO FAR. I'M GOING TO GO SEE THE REAL BAD CRIMINALS TODAY. IT'S JUST SO HARD TO BELIEVE THEY COMMITTED SUCH SERIOUS CRIMES. YOU WOULDN'T KNOW IT WHEN TALKING TO THEM. THEY ARE AWFUL NICE AND FRIENDLY AND WELL EDUCATED. I GUESS IF I WAS TO REALLY TALK TO THEM I'LL KNOW WHATS IN THERE HEART(MATTHEW 15:19).

For out of the heart come evil thoughts, murder, adultery, sexual immorality, theft, false witness, slander.

THESE DEPUTIES SURE HAVE A BAD WAY OF TALKING TO A PERSON AND TREATING THEM IN HERE. THEIR FAVORITE LINE IS, OH WELL IF YOU DON'T LIKE IT DON'T COME BACK TO JAIL. MY BUNK-MATE/CO-WORKER SAID TO ME, I KNOW YOU'LL BE GLAD TO BE LEAVING HERE(JAIL) SOON. I SAID TO BE HONEST, I'M AFRAID. I KEEP SAYING IT, I WANT TO DO THE RIGHT THING SO BAD. IT CAN ONLY HAPPEN IF I PUT GOD FIRST IN MY LIFE. LORD PLEASE LEAD AND I WILL FOLLOW.

I must admit it was hard for me to not eat my lunch tray. But I didn't eat it. I don't know what it is but the lady in commissary insist on me speaking to her today.

I actually rather keep my mouth shut and do my time. If I don't speak, she can make it very hard for me. I really don't need that. The real bad criminals are talking about flooding the floors, I guess it gives them some kind of pleasure or it's because they are not allowed to get commissary. Some of these guys wont see light of day till they go to prison.

Well it's been another blessed day. Lord I thank you for allowing me to see it.

DAY 22

(1 John 5:18)
We know that anyone born of God does not continue to sin; the One who was born of God keeps them safe, and the evil one cannot harm them.

ANOTHER DAY HAS ARRIVED THAT THE LORD HAS BLESSED ME WITH. THIS MORNING I SEEN AN INMATE GO TO REHAB. HE WENT TO THE SAME ONE I'M GOING TO. THAT LETS ME KNOW PEOPLE DO GO TO REHAB FROM HERE(JAIL). I'M ALWAYS WONDERING DO PEOPLE EVEN LEAVE THIS PLACE PERIOD, I KNOW THEY DO BUT I DOUBT EVERYTHING, DUE TO THE FACT THAT I'VE BEEN LET DOWN SO MUCH.

I'M STILL DOING MY FAST, MY BODY IS REALLY GETTING UNDER CONTROL BUT I'M IN HERE(JAIL) SO IT HAS TO BE. I'M GLAD TO KNOW TIME NEVER STOPS, THAT MEANS THE THE CLOSER I GET TO BE RELEASED FROM HERE(JAIL). I HAVE TO REMEMBER THAT OUR TIME IS NOT THE SAME AS GOD'S TIME(2 PETER 3:8):

Don't let it escape your notice, dear friends, that with the Lord a single day is like a thousand years and a thousand years are like a single day.

IN READING THIS SCRIPTURE, I KNOW I DON'T HAVE A WHOLE LOT OF TIME TO GET IT RIGHT WITH GOD, BEFORE JUDGMENT DAY. MY BUNK-MATE/CO-WORKER SAID I WAS JUDGMENTAL, HE MUST HAVE SEEN SOMETHING IN ME OR THINGS I'VE SAID THAT CAUSED HIM TO COME TO THAT CONCLUSION ABOUT ME. I NEEDED THAT THOUGH LORD KNOWS I CAN'T JUDGE NO ONE OR THING (MATTHEW 7:1-2):

Don't judge, so that you won't be judged. **2** You'll receive the same judgment you give. Whatever you deal out will be dealt out to you.

WELL THE OTHER INMATES/TRUSTEES ARE SMOKING WEED AND CRACK ON OUR FLOOR. I'LL REALLY BE STAYING IN MY ROOM TONIGHT. OH IT SUPPOSE TO BE FREE OF DRUGS AND CIGARETTES IN THE JAIL. IT'S ACTUALLY EASIER TO GET DRUGS AND CIGARETTES IN JAIL THAN IT IS IN THE STREETS.

I'VE SEEN THE JAIL TRY THEIR BEST TO KEEP IT OUT, AND THEY DO A VERY GOOD JOB BUT A LOT OF THE PEOPLE IN JAIL ARE VERY SMART BUT JUST MADE DUMB DECISIONS. SO THE INMATES FIGURE OUT WAYS TO GET IT IN. JUST ATE

DINNER TODAY IT WAS OK, I'M DOING OK ON MY FAST. WELL ANOTHER DAY DOWN AND ON TOP OF THAT I'M IN THE SINGLE DIGITS TO THE DATE OF MY RELEASE TO REHAB.

MY EMOTIONS ARE RAGING. WOW!!! JUST WHEN YOU THINK YOU'VE SEEN IT ALL IN HERE(JAIL). SOMETHING ELSE HAPPENS, BUT THIS WAS AWESOME TO SEE. THE INMATES IN THIS POD CAME TOGETHER FOR AN INMATE WHO WAS SMOKING, IN WHICH HE SMELLED LIKE CIGARETTE SMOKE. THE DEPUTY WAS DOING HIS ROUNDS HE SMELLED THE CIGARETTE SMOKE IN HIS ROOM AND ON HIM. THE DEPUTY TOLD HIM TO GIVE UP THE LIGHTER OR BE REMOVED FROM A TRUSTEE BACK TO A REGULAR INMATE, WHICH IS NOT GOOD AT ALL.

EVERYBODY ON THE POD SCRAMBLED TO FIND ANY KIND OF LIGHTER THEY COULD FIND TO SAVE HIS BUTT, IN WHICH THEY CAME UP WITH ONE. JUST GOES TO SHOW YOU THAT EVEN IN HERE(JAIL) PEOPLE DO HAVE A HEART. BUT

STILL WATCH WHO YOU TRUST IN HERE AND ON THE OUTSIDE WORLD. SMILING FACES CAN BE VERY DECEITFUL. WELL THIS DAY IS OVER. I HOPE AND PRAY I'M BLESS TO SEE ANOTHER TOMORROW. LORD I THANK YOU FOR THIS DAY.

DAY 23

(1 John 5:14-15)
This is the confidence that we have in our relationship with God: If we ask for anything in agreement with his will, he listens to us. **15** *If we know that he listens to whatever we ask, we know that we have received what we asked from him.*

I MADE IT TO ANOTHER DAY I'M BLESSED SO BECAUSE THERE ARE SOME PEOPLE WHO DIDN'T WAKE UP TODAY. LORD I THANK YOU.

ACCORDING TO THESE SCRIPTURES, AS LONG AS I HAVE A RELATIONSHIP WITH HIM, I CAN ASK GOD FOR ANYTHING I WANT ACCORDING TO HIS WILL FOR MYSELF. AND KNOW I WILL RECEIVE IT. I'M ASKING HIM TO KEEP HIS ARMS OF PROTECTION AROUND ME AND GUIDE MY PATHWAY.

WELL TODAY IS TRUSTEE LAUNDRY DAY IN WHICH WE WASH ALL THE TRUSTEES LAUNDRY. I MAKE OUT BIG TIME, WITH FOOD AND CANDY BECAUSE I DO THE OTHERS TRUSTEE LAUNDRY PERSONALLY.

I started reading this book call 12 stupid things that mess up recovery, by Allen Berger PHD it's about the mistakes people make while in recovery. So far a couple things that really stuck out to me. This book said addiction is a medical decease with a spiritual cure.

Then said we must die before we can be reborn and we must descend before we can ascend. Oh one more thing the book said was, many people believe that we discover spirituality through pain. Which in a lot of situations is true. This just lets me know even more I need God to help me with my problems and my addiction.

Well nothing really happen today, myself and my co-workers didn't talk much at all. I think we're just tried of looking at each other day in and day out plus every night. So this day just dragged by. I did eat dinner, which wasn't good at all. While

THIS DAY WAS DRAGGING BY, IT MADE ME THINK ABOUT PEOPLE AND THINGS IN MY PAST WHICH HURTS ME TO THINK ABOUT. MY PAST WILL BE A HARD DOOR TO SHUT. NO MATTER HOW HARD I TRY TO CLOSE IT. IT WILL ALWAYS OPEN BACK UP. EITHER BY MYSELF OR PEOPLE CONSTANTLY REMINDING ME OF IT.

I BELIEVE I NEED TO BE REMINDED OF MY PAST IN TO MAKE MY FUTURE BRIGHTER. SURRENDERING, HUMILITY AND ADDICTION ARE THINGS FROM MY PAST, I'M GONNA HAVE TO HURDLE IN ORDER TO HAVE A BRIGHT FUTURE(MATTHEW 23:12).
All who lift themselves up will be brought low. But all who make themselves low will be lifted up.

AGAIN I'M IN JAIL, SO THAT'S WHY I'M SO SPIRITUAL NOW. THE SAYING GOES GOD IS ALL YOU NEED, BECAUSE GOD IS ALL YOU GOT. I WONT BE IN JAIL MY WHOLE LIFE.

LET'S SEE HOW I AM WHEN I LEAVE HERE(JAIL). STATISTIC'S SAY THE AVERAGE PERSON WHO IS RELEASED FROM JAIL OR PRISON. RETURN TO

JAIL OR PRISON WITH 3 MONTHS TO A YEAR OF BEING RELEASED FROM JAIL OR PRISON. THIS IS MAINLY DUE TO THE INDIVIDUAL NOT WANTING TO CHANGE, BEING SUCKED BACK INTO BAD HABITS FROM THEIR ENVIRONMENT BY SUCH PEOPLE AS FAMILY AND FRIENDS, UNABLE TO GET EMPLOYMENT RIGHT AWAY, A PLACE TO CALL HOME ETC. YES THIS IS A LOT ME AND OTHERS HAVE TO HANDLE, BUT IT'S NO EXCUSE. I DO WANT GOD IN MY LIFE(GALATIONS 2:20):

I have been crucified with Christ and I no longer live, but Christ lives in me. And the life that I now live in my body, I live by faith, indeed, by the faithfulness of God's Son, who loved me and gave himself for me.

THIS IS WHAT I NEED TO HELP ME GET OVER OBSTACLES. BUT I ALSO KNOW ABOUT LAW OF ATTRACTION(WHAT YOU THINK ABOUT YOU BRING ABOUT). IN WHICH YOU DON'T HAVE TO BE REALLY SPIRITUAL TO UNDERSTAND. IF A PERSON FOCUSES HIS OR HER MIND ON DOING THE RIGHT THING OR ON ACHIEVING SOMETHING IN LIFE, EVENTUALLY IT WILL COME TO PASS. THAT'S THE WAY OF LAW OF THE UNIVERSE WORKS, IT HAS TO HAPPEN FOR THAT

INDIVIDUAL AND WILL HAPPEN. JUST DON'T GIVE-UP!!!!!!!!!!! SO IF I COME BACK TO JAIL I KNOW IT WILL BE COMPLETELY MY FAULT. I CHOSE TO BASICALLY TO GIVE UP. SEEN SOME OF THE INMATES GET THEIR DRUGS TODAY. NOW TELL ME WHAT KIND OF LESSON ARE THEY'RE BEING TAUGHT. HEY IT'S THEIR LIFE. I HAVE TO SEEK MY OWN SOUL SALVATION(PHILLIPPIANS 2:12).

Therefore, my loved ones, just as you always obey me, not just when I am present but now even more while I am away, carry out your own salvation with fear and trembling.

I'M NOT DOING THE DRUGS. I STILL HAVE MY OWN DEMONS THAT ONLY GOD AND PRAYER CAN HELP. HEY ANOTHER DAY DOWN. LORD I THANK YOU FOR GETTING ME THROUGH ANOTHER DAY.

SEEING A MAN FACING LIFE...

I SERVED FOOD TO A MAN FACING NATRUAL LIFE IN PRISON FOR THE MURDER OF A TODDLER. HOW AND WHY WOULD HE DO THAT TO A CHILD? I HAVE TO TREAT HIM WITH RESPECT OR I'LL GET IN TROUBLE. SEEING HIM AND OTHER REAL BAD CRIMINALS WHO ARE ON THE SAME FLOOR AS HIM GIVES ME A NEW LOOK ON LIFE, SEEING HOW PRECIOUS IT IS. I WILL SEE THE LIGHT OF DAY, HE WILL TO BUT IT WILL BE WITH A FENCE AROUND IT. HE WILL ALWAYS HAVE TO WATCH HIS BACK FOR THE CRIME COMMITTED. TO KILL SOMEONE IS AGAINST THE BIBLE AND THE LAW. SOME ARE JUSTIFIELD BUT MOST ARE NOT.

I'M IN JAIL FOR FAR LESS CRIME BUT TO BE IN JAIL WITH MURDERS WHO I'VE SEEN ON TV THEN SEE THEM IN PERSON JUST BLOWS MY MIND. NO MATTER THE SIZE OF THE CRIME YOU COMMIT, YOU WILL BE TREATED LIKE ALL

INMATES(BAD). THIS FOR SURE IS A LESSON LEARNED. WELL THE BABY KILLER GOT SENTENCE TO LIFE IN PRISON. BUT HE'S GONNA TRY TO APPEAL IT TO A LESSOR CRIME. WTH...

Chapter 4

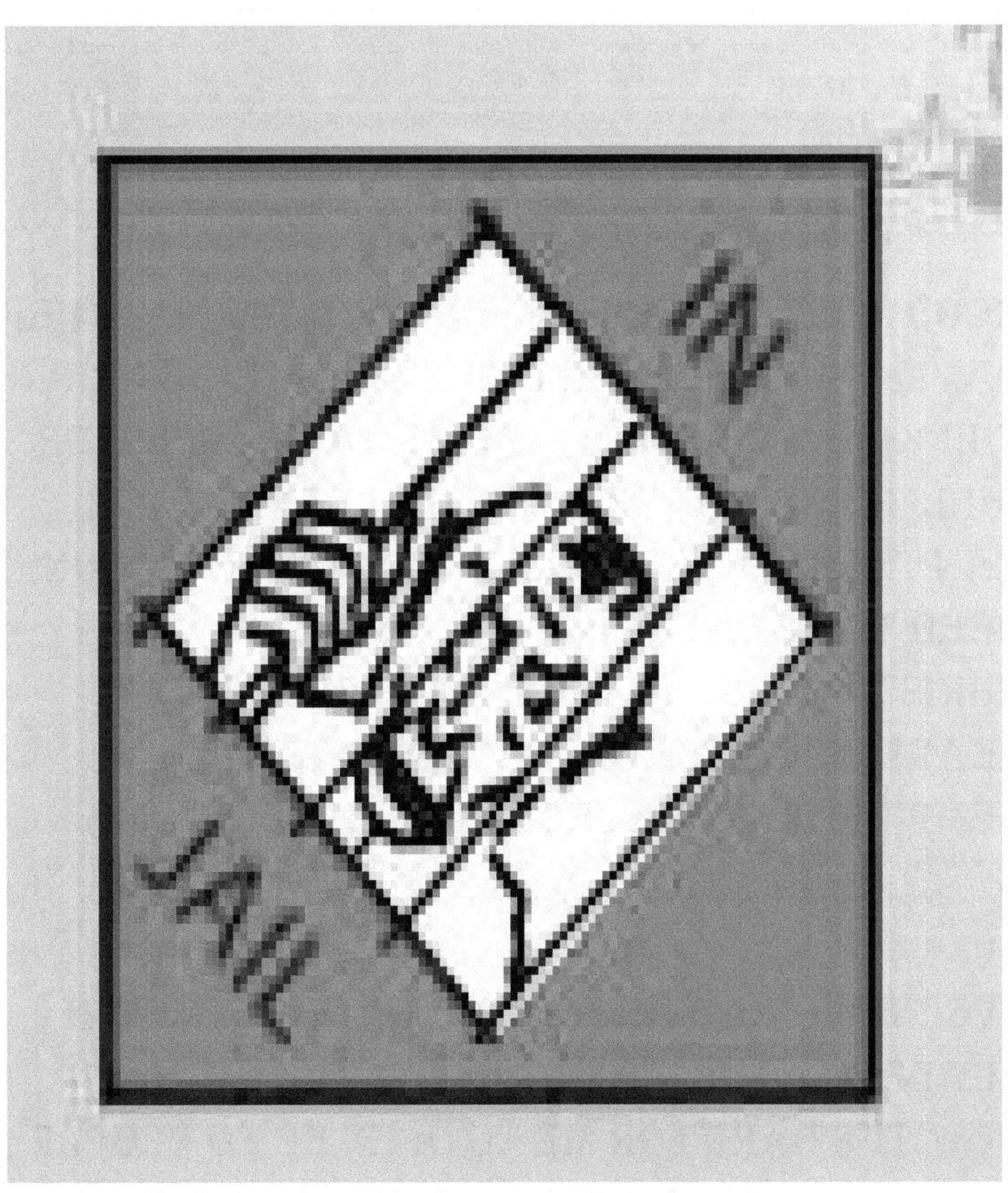

DAY 24

(Galations 6:1-3)

Brothers and sisters, if a person is caught doing something wrong, you who are spiritual should restore someone like this with a spirit of gentleness. Watch out for yourselves so you won't be tempted too. **2** Carry each other's burdens and so you will fulfill the law of Christ. **3** If anyone thinks they are important when they aren't, they're fooling themselves.

(1 John 1:7)

But if we live in the light in the same way as he is in the light, we have fellowship with each other, and the blood of Jesus, his Son, cleanses us from every sin.

GOOD MORNING, THANK YOU LORD FOR ANOTHER DAY. I WAS LAYING IN BED EARLY THIS MORNING THINKING ABOUT HOW I DON'T HAVE A WIFE OR GIRLFRIEND. I HAVE ONE FRIEND THAT I MAY CAN TALK TO WHEN ALL THIS IS OVER. I'M GONNA NEED TO GET ME A CHRISTIAN FRIEND WHO I CAN TELL ALL MY FEARS, WORRIES, CONCERNS AND THE TEMPTATIONS I HAVE (JAMES 5:16):

For this reason, confess your sins to each other and pray for each other so that you may be healed. The prayer of the righteous person is powerful in what it can achieve.

I'VE NEVER HAD ANYONE I CAN TRUST, WHICH LEADS ALL THE WAY BACK TO MY CHILDHOOD TO NOW. IT'S HARD FOR ME TO OPEN UP TO PEOPLE I KNOW, SO YOU CAN IMAGINE HOW HARD IT WILL BE TO OPEN UP TO PEOPLE I'M GETTING TO KNOW.

I'M READING THE BOOK, 12 STEPS THAT MESS UP RECOVERY. THE BOOK KEEPS LETTING ME KNOW I HAVE TO BE HUMBLE. GOD KNOWS THAT'S GONNA BE HARD FOR ME. I KNOW I'M REALLY GONNA HAVE TO SET MY PRIDE ASIDE IN ORDER TO BE A SERVANT FOR GOD (2 CORINTHIANS 6:4):
But as servants of God we commend ourselves in every way: by great endurance, in afflictions, hardships, calamities.

WELL THE TOILET IS NOT FLUSHING IN MY POD. THE OTHER INMATES SAY THEY GONNA REPORT THIS TO THE NEWS WHEN THEY ARE RELEASED, CAUSE THIS IS INHUMANE. I WONT BE EATING TONIGHT CAUSE THAT WILL MAKE ME HAVE TO USE THE BATHROOM. HEY LIKE THE DEPUTIES SAY, DON'T COMEBACK IF YOU DON'T LIKE IT. WELL THIS IS THE END TO ANOTHER DAY AND IT'S A DAY I WON'T HAVE TO DO OVER. NOT EVERYDAY IS EVENTFUL.

LORD THANK YOU FOR GETTING ME THROUGH ANOTHER DAY.

DAY 25

(1 Corinthians 10:23)

No temptation has seized you that isn't common for people. But God is faithful. He won't allow you to be tempted beyond your abilities. Instead, with the temptation, God will also supply a way out so that you will be able to endure it.

THANK YOU LORD FOR ONE MORE DAY IN THE LAND OF THE LIVING. WELL BACK TO THE LAUNDRY FOR ANOTHER DAY(LOL). THIS MORNING IS GOING OK SO FAR. I GOT SOME SLEEP LAST NIGHT EVEN THOUGH THE DEVIL ATTACKED MY MIND BIG=TIME.

I MUST BE DOING SOMETHING RIGHT OR GOING TO DO SOMETHING BIG FOR GOD FOR THE ENEMY(DEVIL)TO ALWAYS ALWAYS ATTACK ME LIKE THIS. HE CAN SEE MY FUTURE MORE THAN I CAN AND IT MUST NOT LOOK GOOD FOR HIM(DEVIL).

I HIT THE JACKPOT TODAY, I GOT MY HANDS ON SOME RIDE OUT CLOTHES. RIDE OUT IS A PERSON WHO HAS LEFT(RIDE OUT) FOR PRISON BUT CAN NOT TAKE HIS OR HER SOCKS,SHOES,UNDERWEAR,T-SHIRTS,TANK

TOPS, WIFE BEATER SHIRTS AND TOP AND BOTTOM LONG JOHNS. I WASH AND BLEACH THE HECK OUT OF THEM TO WEAR THEN I'M GONNA GIVE THEM AWAY WHEN I LEAVE HERE (JAIL). I HAVE TO BE A BLESSING BECAUSE I'VE BEEN BLESSED. WELL AS MY TIME WINDS DOWN HERE (JAIL), THEN THE NEXT STEP IN MY JOURNEY BEGINS.

ALL I CAN DO IS THANK MY HIGHER POWER WHICH FOR ME IS GOD. HE HAD TO PUT ME IN JAIL IN ORDER FOR HIM TO STRAIGHT MY LIFE OUT. AS I LOOK BACK IF I DIDN'T GET INCARCERATED, I WOULD HAVE KILLED MYSELF, ANOTHER PERSON OR BOTH.

THIS IS WHAT HAD TO BE DONE IN ORDER FOR ME TO GET MY LIFE ON THE RIGHT TRACK. I HAD OTHER THINGS AND SITUATIONS THAT SHOULD HAVE HELP ME, BUT THEY DIDN'T. I KNOW IF I GO BACK TO MY OLD WAY, IT ONLY GETS WORST. I'LL BE FACING DEATH.

Not just physical death, but a living death, in which I believe is worst than a physical death.

I read today in the book, the 12 things that mess up recovery. I was reading the amends part of the book to love ones, friends and people I've hurt, which is step 9 in AA/NA. Made direct amends to such people wherever possible, except when to do so would injure them or others.

This step is going to be very hard for me. To "me" it's the hardest of all. I've apologize many times before and still messed up,

I know no one wants to hear what I have to say, I know I wouldn't. But one of the best ways to do this step, is not say a word to all I've harmed. Just start living my life right and not go back to my old ways.

OVER TIME THEY'LL SEE THE CHANGE IN YOU AND START TO ACCEPTED AND CARE FOR YOU AGAIN. BUT YOU WILL HAVE THOSE WHO NEVER ACCEPT YOU, IN FACT THEY'LL BE WAITING FOR YOU TO MESS UP AGAIN, JUST SO THE CAN SAY I TOLD YOU SO. THOSE PEOPLE YOU DON'T NEED IN YOUR LIFE ANYWAY.

WELL NOTHING REALLY HAPPEN TODAY IN LAUNDRY. I JUST READ AND WAS BORED, AND WOULD YOU BELIEVE I'M STILL TIRED.

BUT IT STILL WAS A BLESSED DAY. SO LORD I THANK YOU AND LOVE YOU ALWAYS.

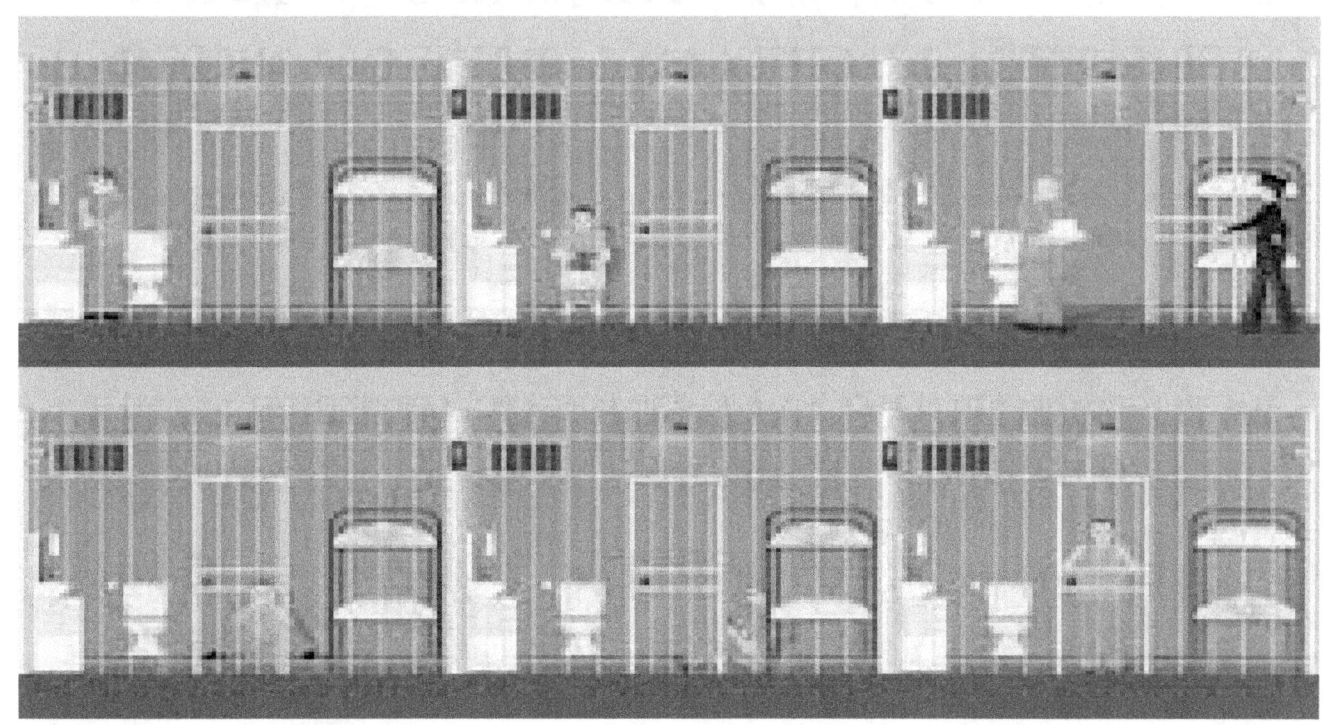

DAY 26

(Isaiah 1:19)
If you are willing and obedient, you will eat the good things of the land.

UP FOR ANOTHER DAY. LORD I THANK YOU FOR THIS DAY YOU BLESS ME WITH. I WAS SUPPOSE TO HAVE HAD THIS DAY OFF, BUT I SOLD IT FOR 2 HONEY BUNS. IT'S OK I HIT THE JACKPOT ON RIDE OUT CLOTHES AGAIN.

WHEN I LEAVE HERE(JAIL), SOMEBODY WILL BE BLESSED. TODAY I'M WORKING WITH THE DIFFICULT CO-WORKER. IT'S BEST I JUST KEEP QUITE AROUND HIM AND IT'S WORKING, NO CONFRONTATION. I'M DETERMINED TO LIVE A DIFFERENT LIFE THEN I WAS LIVING(1 PETER 5:9):

Resist him, standing firm in the faith, because you know that the family of believers throughout the world is undergoing the same kind of sufferings.

I DEFINITELY WILL BE WALKING OUT OF HERE WITH SOMETHING, ALL FOR THE BETTER. WELL MY CO-WORKER IS HAVING HIS ISSUES, BUT OH WELL, I'LL JUST KEEP QUITE. IN WATCHING HIM ALL I CAN SAY IS WOW. SINCE TODAY IS THE

Easiest day of the week, we get done with washing everything early. But we have to stay around here in the laundry room, in which I rather be watching football.

The release date is getting close, this is the last Saturday I will work and work with this co-worker thank God. I'm noticing the old me popping up, which scares me. I really don't want that. Have to thank God for revealing that to me.

I have my mind set a certain way, because I'm in here(jail). That is not to think of things in the outside world because I'm not on the outside. I know when I get out my mind can turn back to the old way at the drop of a dime. My ex-wife said she want to see if I really change. Well today was a reeeeeeeeeeeeeeeeeeeeeeeeeeeeeeeeeeeel boring day. Nothing happen in laundry.

Well good night and Lord I thank you.

DAY 27

(Colossians 3:16)
The word of Christ must live in you richly. Teach and warn each other with all wisdom by singing psalms, hymns, and spiritual songs. Sing to God with gratitude in your hearts.

THIS DAY GOT HERE QUICK. I THANK GOD FOR ANOTHER DAY. I'M GETTING MORE NERVOUS ABOUT THE FUTURE. WELL WE KNOW IN ORDER FOR ME TO MAKE IT OUT THERE, I HAVE TO BE HUMBLE, THAT'S BEEN DRILLED IN MY HEAD. I'M REALLY SEEING THAT MORE AND MORE. I HAVE NOTHING TO BE PRIDEFUL ABOUT I'VE BEEN STRIP DOWN TO NOTHING, THAT MEANS I'M REALLY GONNA LEARN HUMILITY. I WANT A CHRIST CENTERED LIFE PLUS HELP OTHERS IN THE PROCESS.

IN WATCHING THESE MACHINE GO ROUND AND ROUND, I READ THE BEST WAY TO BE A WITNESS FOR CHRIST THAT WILL LEAD PEOPLE TO GODS KINGDOM. IS TO TELL MY STORY OF WHAT GOD HAS DONE FOR ME AND BROUGHT ME THROUGH. IN SHARING MY STORY, I REALLY BELIEVE IT CAN HELP IN

KNOWING IF I CAN MAKE MAKE THEY CAN ALSO, AS LONG AS THEY PUT GOD FIRST IN THEIR LIFE. MY BUNKMATE/CO-WORKER SAID I'M GOOD AT SETTING MY PRIDE ASIDE. HE SAID I'M NOT ASHAME TO TELL PEOPLE I HAVE AN ADDICTION PROBLEM AND MADE A MESS OF MY LIFE(1 TIMOTHY 3:6):

He must not be a recent convert, or he may become conceited and fall under the same judgment as the devil.

I'VE LEARNED IN HERE(JAIL). I CAN'T GO AROUND TRYING TO MAKE LIGHT OF MY PROBLEMS, THAT WOULD BE PRIDE GETTING IN THE WAY. I GOT TO FACE UP TO MY PROBLEMS AND ASK GOD TO GIVE ME THE STRENGTH TO TELL OTHERS OF MY PROBLEMS,
THATS BEING HUMBLE. THIS WILL ALSO HELP WITH MY WALK WITH GOD AND HAVE A MUCH BETTER LIFE. SOON I'LL BE IN REHAB, WHERE I HAVE TO TELL AND DEAL WITH ALL MY ISSUES AND PROBLEMS, NO NEED IN SUGAR COATING THEM. I BELIEVE AFTER THE FIRST TIME I TELL MY STORY, IT WILL BE DOWNHILL FROM THERE.

THE HARD PART WILL BE OPENING UP TO TELL MY STORY. I KNOW MY HIGHER POWER(GOD) WILL GET ME PAST MY FEAR OF OPENING UP. ALL THE RELATIONSHIPS I'VE BEEN IN HAVE BEEN DYSFUNCTIONAL WHICH HAVE AND CAUSE ME TO RELAPSE. BUT NO MATTER THE RELATIONSHIP, I STILL HAD A CHOICE AND I CHOSE WRONG AND LOOK WHERE IT GOT ME.

RIGHT NOW I CAN'T THINK OF A RELATIONSHIP RIGHT NOW, I HAVE TO FOCUS ON ME BEFORE I CAN BRING SOMEONE ELSE INTO IT. NO MATTER A RELATIONSHIP IS DOWN THE ROAD. WELL NOT MUCH ACTION TODAY IN LAUNDRY LAND. GONNA GO BACK TO MY POD

TO REST, READ AND THEN SLEEP. WELL HOPE I'M ALIVE TO WRITE TOMORROW, IF NOT, LORD I THANK YOU FOR MY TIME ON EARTH..

DAY 28

(Hebrews 12:2-3)

Fixing our eyes on Jesus, the pioneer and perfecter of faith. For the joy set before him he endured the cross, scorning its shame, and sat down at the right hand of the throne of God. **3** *Consider him who endured such opposition from sinners, so that you will not grow weary and lose heart.*

Here it is 3 days left to my life changing journey. God works in 3's. For example, Noah had three sons (Gen 6:10) and Job had three daughters (Job 1:2; cf. 42:13); The Ark of the Covenant contained three sacred objects 'The gold jar of manna, Aaron's staff that had budded, and the stone tablets of the covenant" (Heb. 9:4). Solomon's Palace of the Forest of Lebanon was designed with windows "placed high in sets of three facing each other. All the doorways had rectangular frames; they were in the front part in sets of three, facing each other" (1 Kgs 7:4-5).Likewise, in John's vision a triple entrance way marked all four sides of the city of the New Jerusalem (Rev 21:13). David "bowed down before Jonathan three times, with his face to the ground" (1 Sam 20:41) and Daniel regularly prayed three times a day giving thanks to God (Dan 6:10, 13). Israelite men were required to appear before the Lord three times in a year: "Three times a year all your men must appear before the LORD your God at the place he will choose: at the Feast of Unleavened Bread, the Feast of Weeks and the Feast of Tabernacles" (Deut 16:16). Jesus answered Satan's threefold temptation by citing three scriptural passages Matt 4:1-11). Paul experienced three shipwrecks (2 Cor 11:28) and prayed three times to the Lord for the removal of his "thorn in the flesh" (2 Cor 12:7-8).

THESE ARE SOME EXAMPLES OF HOW GOD PERFORM THINGS AND SITUATIONS IN 3'S. ACCORDING TO THESES SCRIPTURES(ABOVE), I CAN USES JESUS AS MY EXAMPLE, HE NEVER LOOKED AT THE CURRENT SITUATION HE WAS IN, BUT FOCUSED ON WHAT WAS AHEAD OF HIM, WHICH WAS GREAT JOY AND BE PUT ON A THRONE. HE JUST HAD TO ENDURE AND KEEP THE FAITH. I'M GONNA USE HIM AS MY FOCAL POINT WHEN ISSUES ARISES, THAT CAUSE ME PAIN, SORROW,SHAME,HURT AND EMBARRASSMENT. I MUST SAY I'M NERVOUS NOW. SOME PEOPLE HAVE BUTTERFLY IN THEIR STOMACH I HAVE

EAGLES(LOL). TODAY WILL BE A BUSY DAY IN LAUNDRY, WHICH WILL MAKE THE DAY GO BY QUICKER. NO BREAKFAST AND LUNCH TODAY. WHICH IS HELPING MORE WHEN THE DEVIL ATTACKS ME, WHICH IS A LOT.

I HELP MY BUNK-MATE/CO-WORKER WRITE A LETTER TO HIS MOTHER TODAY. HE'S TRYING TO MEND A BROKEN RELATIONSHIP. I TALKED TO HIM ABOUT HOW I HAVE REGRETS WHEN IT COMES TO MY MOTHER. SHE PAST NEVER KNOWING IF I LOVED HER. I TOLD HIM NOT TO MAKE THE SAME MISTAKES I DID.

WISH MY MOTHER AND I HAD WORKED OUT OUR DIFFERENCES BEFORE SHE PASSED. WHICH BOTHERS ME EVERYDAY OF MY LIFE. WELL HE HAS TAKING HEED TO WHAT I TOLD HIM, THANK GOD. THIS DAY HAS FLOWN BY. BESIDES THE DEVIL ATTACKING ME, IT'S BEEN A BUSY DAY. I KNOW WHAT I HAVE TO DO, THAT IS KEEP THE FAITH(2 CORINTHIANS 5:7):

For we live by faith, not by sight.

As my stay here is coming to an end. I'm thanking God for the lesson learned and the knowledge gained. I needed this to put me on the right path before it was too late. God has a plan for me and my future.

I know if I stay on this path it will lead others to God's kingdom and a fulfilling and blessed life. I believe when people see the change in me, they will realize they can change also. An inmate just came to me and said, it's easy to be cured in jail. But what about when you get out. He is so right.

That's why I'm working on my defenses while in here. I know the horrible pain I went through and the pain I caused others because of my addiction. I don't wont this anymore. I've said that a lot in the past.

God first back then, will now (Matthew 6:33):
But seek first his kingdom and his righteousness, and all these things will be given to you as well.

WELL I THANK YOU LORD I THANK YOU, FOR ANOTHER DAY. IF I DIE BEFORE I WAKE, I PRAY THE LORD MY SOUL TO TAKE.

DAY 29

(John 15:5)
I am the vine; you are the branches. If you remain in me and I in you, you will bear much fruit; apart from me you can do nothing.

(2 Corinthians 12:9-10)
But he said to me, "My grace is sufficient for you, for my power is made perfect in weakness." Therefore I will boast all the more gladly about my weaknesses, so that Christ's power may rest on me. **10** That is why, for Christ's sake, I delight in weaknesses, in insults, in hardships, in persecutions, in difficulties. For when I am weak, then I am strong.

(Philippians 4:13)
I can do all this through him who gives me strength.

(Hebrews 13:6)
So we say with confidence.

THE LORD IS MY HELPER; I WILL NOT BE AFRAID. WHAT CAN MERE MORTALS DO TO ME? LORD I THANK YOU FOR ANOTHER DAY YOU ALLOW ME TO SEE. WHAT I GOT FROM THESE SCRIPTURES, NO MATTER WHAT I'M FACING WHATS AHEAD OF ME. SUCH AS PUT DOWNS, LAUGHTER AIM AT ME, SHAME, HOMELESSNESS, FEAR, PAINS, TURN DOWNS, BEING UNWANTED, NO MONEY AND LOTS OF NEGATIVE SITUATIONS.

WITH GOD HAVING MY BACK, I WILL COME OUT ON TOP. SO LORD I THANK YOU IN ADVANCE. WOW!!!

2 DAYS LEFT TO MY STAY HERE, THEN TO REHAB. I'M GETTING BUBBLE GUTS OR JUST PLAIN NERVOUS. GOT UP THIS MORNING DID MY DAILY READING OF RICK WARRENS PURPOSE DRIVEN LIFE. WHICH IS AN AWESOME BOOK. READ SOMETHING IN IT TODAY THAT BLEW ME AWAY. IT SAID MY LIFE IS A JOURNEY. I SHOULD WRITE DOWN MY FEARS, PAINS, STRUGGLES AND DOUBTS. THEN TELL HOW GOD TURN THEM INTO FULFILLMENT OF MY PURPOSE IN LIFE FOR HIS GLORY(GOD). THE ENEMY AS BEEN ATTACKING ME BIG-TIME ABOUT WRITING THIS BOOK. THAT JUST LETS ME KNOW I'M ON THE RIGHT TRACK AND DOING SOMETHING GOOD FOR GODS PURPOSE. IT'S A MUST I PASS ON MY KNOWLEDGE TO FUTURE GENERATIONS, IT'S MY RESPONSIBILITY(PSALMS 102:18).

Let this be written for a future generation, that a people not yet created may praise the Lord

MY STOMACH IS IN KNOTS. I'M WAITING FOR MY CASE WORKER TO MEET WITH ME TODAY BUT I HAVE A FEELING SHE WON'T SHOW UP TODAY. IN JAIL YOU LEARN A LOT OF DEPUTIES AND JAIL

WORKERS LIE TO YOU A AWFUL LOT, SO WHEN THEY SAY THEY GOING TO DO SOMETHING FOR YOU. 9 TIMES OUT OF 10 THEY WILL NOT DO WHAT THEY SAID THEY WAS GOING TO DO. WHEN YOU ASK THEM DID THEY DO WHAT YOU ASK OF THEM TO DO, THEIR REPLY IS THEY HAVEN'T GOT AROUND TO IT YET. WHAT CAN YOU DO? ABSOLUTELY NOTHING. THEIR FAMOUS SAYING IS: DON'T COME HERE(JAIL) OR BACK. MATTHEW 6:34 SAYS:

Therefore do not worry about tomorrow, for tomorrow will worry about itself. Each day has enough trouble of its own.

I JUST HAVE TO DO WHAT THE SCRIPTURE SAYS BUT IT'S VERY HARD. I AM GETTING BETTER AT IT THOUGH. I'M HAVING THE FAITH IN KNOWING ALL THIS IS IN GODS PLAN FOR MY LIFE. I HAVE TO STEP BACK AND LET HIM(GOD) HANDLE IT(HEBREWS 10:39).

NOW, WE DO NOT BELONG TO THOSE WHO TURN BACK AND ARE DESTROYED, BUT TO THOSE WHO HAVE FAITH AND ARE SAVED.

I JUST DON'T WANT A REPEAT OF BEFORE(PAST). I'LL BE LEAVING HERE IN 2 DAYS, I JUST HAVE TO BE PATIENT(HEBREWS

6:12):
Then, instead of being lazy, you will imitate those who are inheriting the promises through faith and patience.

GOD THIS IS IN YOUR HANDS. ONE OF THE 3 GOOD DEPUTIES THAT DO CARE, DID CALL MY CASE MANAGER'S OFFICE FOR ME AND TALKED TO HER BOSS. SHE SAID SHE HERSELF WAS GOING TO COME ME TOMORROW AND SEND AN EMAIL TO MY CASE MANAGER. AGAIN I'M PRETTY SURE I WON'T SEE HER TOMORROW.

I JUST KNOW GODS GONNA WORK THIS OUT FOR ME. MY BUNK-MATE/CO-WORKER GOT INTO A BIG ARGUMENT WITH THE OTHER WORKER WITH US, WHO I GOT INTO IT WITH, HE REALLY KNOWS HOW TO RUB A PERSON THE WRONG WAY. AFTER OUR ALTERCATION, I SAID I'M NOT GOING TO LET HIM GET TO ME EVER AGAIN, WE'VE CAME CLOSE TO BLOWS BUT GOD KEPT ME CALM AND DEFUSED THE SITUATION. WHEN I GO BACK TO MY POD, I'M GONNA GET MY THINGS TOGETHER

I'LL BE TAKING WITH ME. I'M GONNA LEAVE LOTS OF CLOTHING AND FOOD FOR THE LESS BLESSED THAN MYSELF. WOW!!! TOMORROW IS THE LAST DAY OF THE COUNTDOWN. THEN MY NEXT STEP IN MY JOURNEY IS REHAB. AFTER REHAB THAT'S WHEN I REALLY HAVE TO DO WHAT I BEEN SAYING ALL THREW THIS BOOK. I KNOW WHAT I HAVE TO DO TO HAVE A BLESS LIFE FROM GOD. I REALLY WANT THIS MORE THAN ANYTHING/EVER.

I'VE HURT PEOPLE'S LIVES, NOW I WANT TO ENRICH PEOPLE'S LIVES BY LEADING THEM TO GODS KINGDOM WHICH WILL LEAD THEM TO A GREAT LIFE HERE ON EARTH. I DO HAVE TO ADMIT IF I DON'T MEET WITH MY CASE MANAGER TOMORROW AND LEAVE WHEN I'M SUPPOSE TO LEAVE, I'LL BE EXTERMELY MAD AND HURT, BUT I'LL ACCEPT IT AND KNOW IT'S HAS TO BE A REASON FOR THIS HAPPENING TO ME. I KNOW IT'S GODS WILL NOT MY OWN WILL
(MATTHEW 6:10):

May your kingdom come. May your will be done, on earth as it is in heaven.

WHEN I AIM RELEASED FROM HERE(JAIL), I'M SO WORRIED AND AFRAID OF WHAT I'M FACING AND UP AGAINST. TO BE REALLY HONEST I DON' WON'T TO GO THROUGH THIS BUT IT'S FOR GODS GLORY(MATTHEW 26:39).

Going on a little farther, he fell on his face and prayed, "O my Father, if it is possible, let this cup pass from me. Yet not what I want but what you want.

It all has a reason(Jeremiah 29:11).

For I know the plans that I have for you,' declares the Lord, 'plans for well-being, and not for calamity, in order to give you a future and a hope.

SO NO MATTER WHAT, LORD I THANK YOU IN ADVANCE AND FOR THIS DAY YOU BLESS ME WITH.

EVE OF MY 30TH DAY COUNTDOWN...

THIS IS THE DAY BEFORE(EVE)MY 30 DAY COUNTDOWN. YOU WOULDN'T BELIEVE THE THINGS I HAVE GOING THROUGH MY HEAD. I'VE BEEN CALLED REVEREND IKE TODAY BY A OLDER MAN IN HIS 60'S. HE DON'T BELIEVE IN THE BIBLE. SO I LEAVE THAT ALONE BUT FOR HIM TO CALL ME REVEREND IKE, I MUST BE DOING SOMETHING RIGHT. BESIDES THAT I HAVE MORE IMPORTANT ISSUES
TO WORRY ABOUT. AS THE DAYS DRAW CLOSER TO MY END OF BEING HERE(JAIL).I GET MORE NERVOUS,WORRIED,AND SCARED. I JUST DON'T WANT TO MESS-UP ANYMORE.

WHEN I LEAVE HERE(JAIL),I'M TO GO TO REHAB FOR AT LEASE 90 DAYS. WHEN I LEAVE THERE,I PRETTY MUCH DON'T HAVE ANYWHERE TO GO, EX-WIFE DON'T WANT ME ANYMORE IN WHICH I DON'T BLAME HER. I'VE CAUSE HER SO MUCH PAIN IN WHICH SHE WILL NEVER GET OVER BECAUSE THE WOUNDS ARE SO DEEP. IT WILL

TAKE A COMPLETE ACT OF GOD FOR HER TO TOTALLY FORGIVE ME, GOD MUST BE DOING SOMETHING TO HER SHE HAS HELP ME OUT BIG TIME SINCE I BEEN IN HERE (JAIL). I LEFT HER FOR ANOTHER WOMAN WHO WAS MARRIED. WELL THAT HAPPEN AND SHE STILL WITH HER HUSBAND.

SHE KEPT IN CONTACT WITH ME FOR A LITTLE OVER A MONTH, THEN TOLD THE MY EX-WIFE SHE REALIZED HOW MUCH SHE LOVED HER HUSBAND AND SHE HAD BEEN WITH HIM SINCE HIGH SCHOOL WHICH IS A TOTAL LIE. SHE BLOCKED MY CALLS FROM JAIL AND GOT HER CELL PHONE NUMBER CHANGED. I CAN SAY MORE BUT I WON'T. TO SUM IT ALL UP, I MESSED UP, I SAY IT WAS A MISTAKE BUT IT WASN'T CAUSE I KNEW WHAT I WAS DOING.

THE BIBLE SAYS YOU REAP WHAT YOU SOW IN OTHER WORDS KARMA. I'M REAPING A HARVEST, NOT IN A GOOD WAY. SOMETHINGS ARE UNAVOIDABLE CHRISTIAN OR NOT. GOD DID

LOOK OUT FOR ME ON THIS CASE. I SHOULD HAVE BEEN GOING TO PRISON IN WHICH I DID NOT. I ALSO WENT FROM NOT HARDLY EATING TO HAVING TOO MUCH TO EAT TO THE POINT I GIVE FOOD AWAY. AT THIS POINT IN MY LIFE I DON'T WONT TO HURT ANYBODY ANYMORE. I HAVE THOUGHT ABOUT GIVING UP AND END IT ALL BUT I CAN'T LET THE DEVIL WIN CAUSE THAT'S WHAT HE WANTS TO DO IS KILL ME. A LOT OF MY DEMONS HELP PUT ME IN THIS SITUATION. IN READING BIBLE AND OTHER CHRISTIAN BOOKS.

ALL MY PAST, PRESENT AND FUTURE IS FOR GODS GLORY. ONCE I PUT GOD FIRST IN MY LIFE. I WILL BE BLESS AND BE A BLESSING TO OTHERS. I'M AT MY VERY BOTTOM. BUT I'M THANKING GOD FOR THIS. BECAUSE I KNOW HOW THIS IS GOING TO END. SO LORD I'M THANKING YOU IN ADVANCE (1 THESSOLONIANS 5:16-18):

16 Rejoice evermore.
17 Pray without ceasing.
18 In every thing give thanks: for this is the will of God in Christ Jesus concerning you.

CONCLUSION

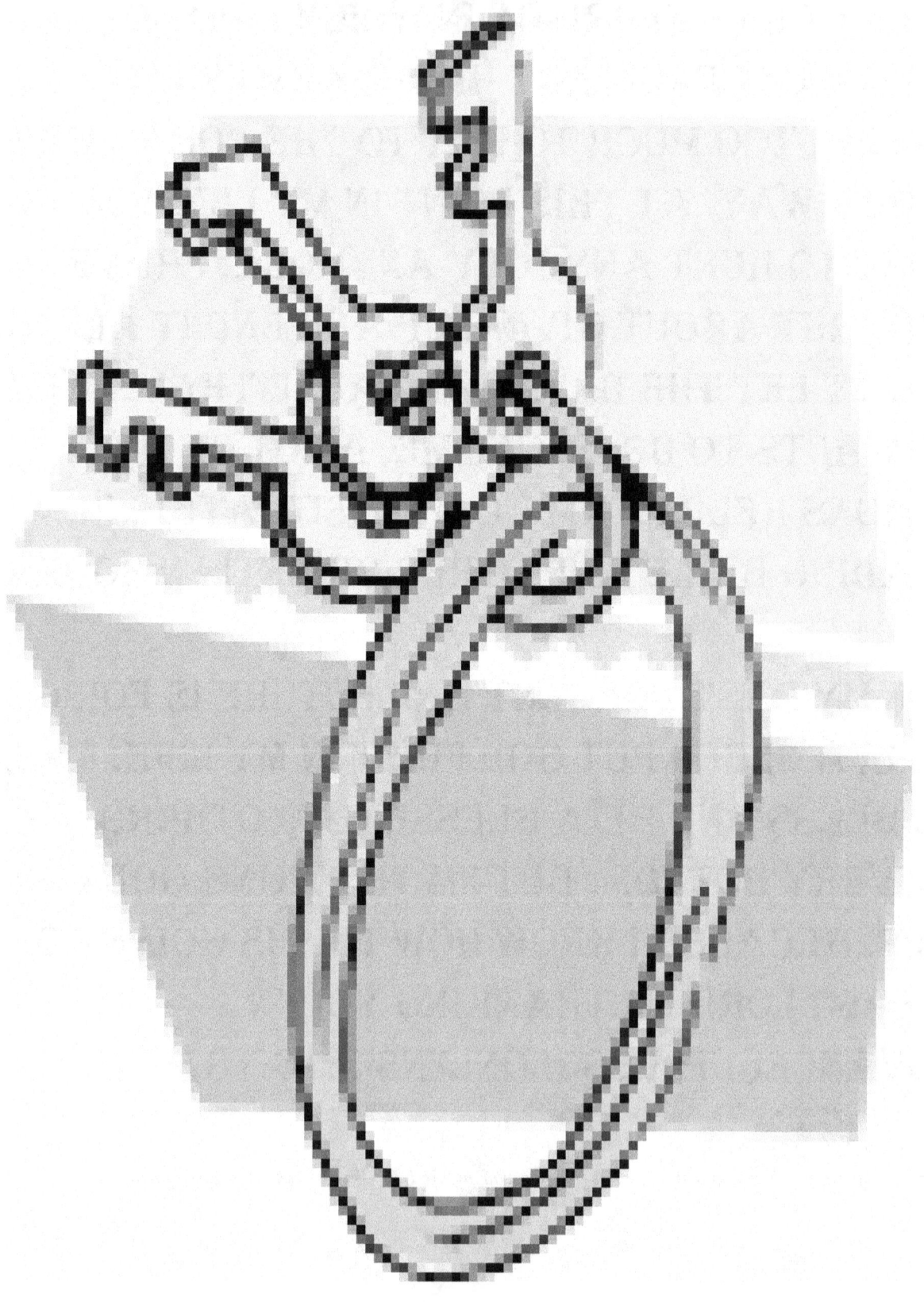

DAY 30

The last day of the countdown

(Matthew 16:24-26)
Then Jesus told his disciples, "If anyone wants to follow me, he must deny himself, pick up his cross, and follow me continuously. **25** Whoever wants to save his life will lose it, but whoever loses his life for my sake will find it, **26** because what profit will a person have if he gains the whole world and forfeits his life? Or what can a person give in exchange for his life?

(1 John 4:18)
There is no fear where love exists. Rather, perfect love banishes fear, for fear involves punishment, and the person who lives in fear has not been perfected in love.

IT'S HERE, ON TOP OF BEING BLESSED TO SEE ANOTHER DAY, THIS IS THE LAST DAY OF THE COUNTDOWN/INCARCERATION. AFTER READING THESE SCRIPTURES, I KNOW I CAN'T BE FEARFUL IN FOLLOWING CHRIST, BECAUSE FOLLOWING HIM IS NOT PUNISHMENT. IT'S ME GAINING A NEW LIFE IN CHRIST. WHICH IS A BLESSED AND FULFILLING ON EARTH THEN ETERNAL LIFE. LORD I THANK YOU FOR THAT. ONLY DIRECTION I NEED IN MY LIFE IS GODS DIRECTION.

(Proverbs 17:24):
A person with understanding has wisdom as his objective, but a fool looks only to earthly goals.

WOW... I JUST READ IF YOU WORRY GOD IS NOT AT THE CENTER OF YOUR LIFE. IF HE WAS, YOU WOULDN'T WORRY BUT WORSHIP HIM. WHAT I'M

ABOUT TO FACE I NEED HIM AT THE CENTER OF MY LIFE NOT ON THE SIDE LOOKING IN. WELL I'M SITTING IN THE
LAUNDRY ROOM BEING NERVOUS WAITING ON CASE MANAGER TO SHOW UP. I'M CLEANING THE SHOES I'M GIVING AWAY WHEN I LEAVE HERE(JAIL). THE DAY IS MOVING RIGHT ALONG BUT STILL NO CASE WORKER. IT LOOKS LIKE I SAID BEFORE, IN JAIL EVEN THE WORKERS LIE TO YOU.

I THOUGHT JAIL STOOD FOR JUST ANOTHER INMATE LYING. WELL I DON'T THINK SO IF YOU ASK ME, THE WORKERS IN JAIL SHOULD BE IN THERE SOMEWHERE. LOOKS LIKE SOMETHING IS GOING TO GO WRONG BUT I'M PREPARED. THE CASE MANAGER DIDN'T SHOW UP. ONE OF THE CARING DEPUTIES CALL DOWN TO THEIR OFFICE, SHE WAS NOT THERE. BUT THE OTHER OFFICE SAID I'M ALL SET FOR RELEASE TOMORROW.

GOD WORKED IT OUT. O.M.G NOW I'M REALLY NERVOUS, TOMORROW STARTS THE NEXT STEP IN MY JOURNEY. I WILL TAKE REHAB REAL SERIOUS THIS TIME. GOD STILL WILL COME FIRST THEN REHAB. IT'S GOING TO BE WEIRD LEAVING HERE (JAIL).

LIKE I SAID BEFORE, EVERYBODY THAT GOES TO JAIL OR PRISON ARE NOT CRIMINALS. A LOT OF THEM ARE GOOD PEOPLE BUT JUST MADE BAD CHOICES. IT KINDA BRING TEARS TO MY EYES. WELL TOMORROW IT WILL BE OFFICIAL, THE NEXT PHASE OF MY JOURNEY BEGINS. GOD & RECOVERY ARE 1ST & 2ND NOW IN MY LIFE.

GOD PUT ME HERE FOR A REASON. NOW THAT I HAVE A CLEAN SLATE, I CAN BE ABOUT GODS BUSINESS. MY WAY WAS FILLED WITH HEARTACHE AND MISERY. NOW I WANT A VERY FULFILLING LIFE, THAT CAN ONLY BE ACHIEVED THROUGH CHRIST. I HOPE THIS BOOK AS TOUCHED YOUR LIFE. I REALLY WANT TO HELP THOSE WHO HAVE BEEN IN IT'S SITUATION.

LORD I PRAY THIS BOOK JUST TOUCH AT LEASE ONE LIFE IF NOT MORE. IF THIS BOOK ONLY TOUCHES ONE LIFE, THAT'S ONE LESS PERSON GOING TO HELL!!.
WELL GOODNIGHT AND I LOVE YOU LORD.

LEAVING DAY

Well I'm really nervous. I'm sitting in holding cell of the jail, waiting for the rehabilitation center to pick me up in there company van. Sitting here watching people come in. I remember when I came in here (jail).

I was really sad and wanting to die. I'm sitting here listening to a guy who is facing 10 years in prison after he was found guilty on his case, now he has to wait for sentencing. He was caught with a lot of pills. He thinks he got the shaft. I'm sure he telling half truths, but that's his life. We all have our own journey. I hope and pray I never come back here again.

As long as I follow the path that God has laid out for me, I'll never ever see this place again. Well it's been a couple hours

NOW AND STILL NO REHABILITATION VAN. I'M SITTING HERE LISTENING TO THESE PEOPLE TELL OF THEIR CASES WHICH IS VERY INTERESTING. THEY ALWAYS SAY WHAT THEY GONNA DO, WHEN THEY KNOW AND THE PEOPLE WHO THEY TALKING TO KNOW THEY NOT GOING TO DO WHAT THEY SAY. THIS IS GOD SHOWING WHAT CAN HAPPEN IF I DON'T FOLLOW HIS PATH THAT HE IS GOING TO LAY OUT FOR ME.

THIS ONE GUY IS REALIZING WHATS ABOUT TO HAPPEN TO HIM, HE MAY NOT GET OUT TILL HE'S OVER 60. HE'S LIKE MID 40'S NOW, HE WANTS TO CRY BIG TIME. I CAN IMAGINE THAT FEELING, TALK ABOUT REALITY.

I CAN NEVER OR WANT TO FORGET THIS EXPERIENCE. CUTTING MY I.D. WRISTBAND OFF REPRESENTED A CHANGE IN MY LIFE AND FUTURE. IT'S A NEW BEGINNING FOR ME NOW. I THANK GOD FOR ANOTHER SHOT AT IT. I BELIEVE THIS IS MY LAST SHOT.

NOW THE JOURNEY BEGINS(PHILIPPIANS 3:13-14):

Brothers, I do not consider myself to have embraced it yet.[b] But this one thing I do: Forgetting what lies behind and straining forward to what lies ahead, **14** *I keep pursuing the goal to win the prize[c] of God's heavenly call in the Messiah[d] Jesus.*

JAIL SUMMARY

TO SUM THIS JAIL EXPERIENCE ALL UP. I CAN'T SAY IT ENOUGH, JAIL IS NOT A PLACE FOR A HUMAN BEINGS. IT'S VERY INHUMANE. YOUR CAGE UP LIKE ANIMALS, TALK TO LIKE ROACHES. I MUST SAY THOUGH, SOME PEOPLE BELONG IN JAIL AND NEVER SEE THE LIGHT OF DAY, UNLESS GOD HAS GOTTEN A HOLD OF THEM. I'VE LEARNED THAT EVERYONE THAT GOES TO JAIL IS NOT A CRIMINAL. I CAN HONESTLY SAY I'VE LEARNED MY LESSON.

AS LONG AS I PUT GOD FIRST IN MY LIFE, I'LL NEVER SEE THIS PLACE AGAIN. THAT'S ANOTHER THING, I'VE SEEN AT LEASE 9 INMATES LEAVE AND RETURN TO JAIL. THEN TO HEAR OTHER INMATES BRAGGING HOW MANY TIMES THEY HAVE LEFT AND RETURNED TO JAIL. THEN ON TOP OF THAT, THE INMATES WHO ARE NOW INCARCERATED, ARE TALKING ABOUT WHEN THEY RETURN AFTER THIS CURRENT INCARCERATION. THAT IS SAD BUT A WAY OF

LIFE FOR THEM. WHEN I EVEN THINK ABOUT RETURNING BACK TO JAIL IT MAKES ME SICK TO MY STOMACH AND FEAR OVERCOMES ME. FEAR WILL SUBSIDE, THAT'S WHY I HAVE TO HAVE SOMETHING IN PLACE SO I DON'T RETURN TO JAIL.

THAT SOMETHING IS GOD. FOR THE OTHER INMATES I HOPE THEY FIND SOMETHING IF NOT GOD. JAIL IS NO PLACE TO BE. BUT IT WAS THE PLACE TO BE FOR GOD TO GET MY ATTENTION. NOW I KNOW MY PURPOSE IN LIFE AND WHAT GOD WANTS FROM ME. ME BEING INCARCERATED WAS ALL FOR A REASON JERMIAH 29:11 SAYS:

For I know the plans I have for you," declares the Lord, "plans to prosper you and not to harm you, plans to give you hope and a future.

SO LORD I THANK YOU. WHILE I WAS INCARCERATED JOAN RIVERS, ROBIN WILLIAMS AND BRUCE MORTON DIED. WHICH REALLY TOUCHED ME, BECAUSE I GREW UP WATCHING THESE PEOPLE ON T.V. THERE ALSO WAS A 50 YEAR REMEMBRANCE OF THE
BEATLES COMING TO MY STATE. ALL OF THIS IS

A LEARNING EXPERIENCE. IT TOOK ME A LONG TIME TO REALIZE WHAT I WANT OUT OF LIFE. I THANK GOD I DID FIND OUT. I WILL USE THIS AS A LESSON TO USE FOR THE REST OF MY LIFE. SO LORD I THANK YOU.

REHAB

As part of my sentence. I had to do in-patient rehabilitation treatment. I was release to a treatment center, I still was basically still in jail but with way more freedom, better food, I wore regular street clothes instead of jail issued clothes. It was a lot better than being in the actual jail. I just couldn't go outside unless it was authorized.

I had to attend classes everyday with weekends free for myself and family visits. I learned a lot in that treatment center that I use to this day. I even got a job in there. My main vocus was to make a better life for myself, once I'm completely free.

EVERYDAY I SAID TO MYSELF I WASN'T GOING TO BE IN THIS SAME SITUATION NEXT YEAR THIS TIME. I WILL BE LIVING A BLESSED LIFE. NOW REMEMBER I LOST EVERYTHING. I HAD NO WIFE, NO GIRL FRIEND, NO CAR, NO HOME BUT I KNEW AND BELIEVED, EVERYTHING WAS GONNA WORKOUT FOR MY GOOD. I STILL READ THE BIBLE EVERYDAY AND KEPT THE FAITH.

NOTE:

THE BOOK OF PROVERBS HAS 31 CHAPTERS. I READ A CHAPTER A DAY, FOR EACH DAY OF THE MONTH. EXAMPLE; FOR THE FIRST DAY OF THE MONTH, I READ CHAPTER 1, FOR THE SECOND DAY OF THE MONTH I READ CHAPTER 2 ETC. THE CHAPTERS ARE NOT LONG AT ALL. YOU DON'T HAVE TO BE RELIGIOUS OR BELIEVE IN GOD TO READ THE BOOK OF PROVERBS. YOU'LL FIND EVERYTHING YOU WANT TO KNOW AND GAIN MUCH KNOWLEDGE TO HELP YOU IN EVERYDAY LIFE IN THIS BOOK.

No matter where you are at in your journey of life. This is a very good habit for everyday life.

As fate would have it. There was a mix up in my paperwork. So I was set for release from the treatment center sooner than ordered. Oh my god!!!!! I was happy and afraid all at the same time. I was happy to be leaving and start living my life. But I was afraid. I would do good for a little while then fall back into my old ways. Which I didn't want.

Also remember I have no place to go. The treatment center got me into a intense out-patient treatment program near my ex-wife house, which also has housing for it's patients. As the release day drew near more fear creeped in. All the books I read along with all the teachings I received was going to be put to use.

ON RELEASE DAY MY EX-WIFE CAME TO PICK ME UP, TO TAKE ME TO THE OUT-PATIENT TREATMENT CENTER. BUT BEFORE I GO THERE. I HAVE TO MEET WITH MY PROBATION OFFICER(P.O.). HE WENT OVER THE GUIDELINES OF MY PROBATION. HE INFORMED ME I WAS ON 3 YEARS INTENSE PROBATION. I ALSO WAS REQUIRED TO WEAR A TETHER FOR 6 MONTHS. MY PROBATION WAS SO STRICT, TO THE POINT IF I MAKE ONE MISTAKE. I COULD END BACK UP IN JAIL. THIS IS WHY MOST INMATES RATHER DO THE FULL JAIL TIME WITH NO PROBATION AFTERWARDS. THEY KNOW THEY'RE GOING TO MESS UP AND END BACK UP IN JAIL. AS YOU CAN SEE. I'M STILL NOT OFF THE HOOK YET.

MY EX-WIFE DROP ME OFF AT THE OUT-PATIENT TREATMENT CENTER WHERE I'LL BE STAYING. IT WAS JUST LIKE THE IN-PATIENT TREATMENT. WITH WEEKENDS OFF AND WAS ABLE TO ACQUIRE A JOB.

This is a federally funded program. In order to stay in the program. You basically have to relapse to receive more funding for your treatment and stay.

I eventually was released from the program because I wasn't relapsing in order to receive funding. I lived with my ex-wife while looking for a job. Not only did I find a job, I ended up with two jobs one full time and one part-time.

Which led me to find ing my own place to live and was able to buy a vehicle. I did get into some trouble with the law while on probation. Because I had paid all my court fees and did relatively well living on my own by having my own place and two jobs. I wasn't put back in jail. I went on to working four jobs on a weekly basis.

which did for about four years. That kept me busy and out of trouble. I'm living in my own apartment, working a decent job. I have an online businesses a online, attend church on a regular basis, so I don't forget who brought me across.

I still focus everyday on my higher power to help me get through my struggles, which I have almost every day. It's my hope that this book will give you hope and faith and believe that you can do this and make a better life for you and your loved ones good luck...

www.ingramcontent.com/pod-product-compliance
Lightning Source LLC
Chambersburg PA
CBHW060500010526
44118CB00018B/2476